MW00412910

Who knew that comedy would
Leonard's book, *Holy Leadership*
wife, businesswoman, and even
the help of the Holy Spirit. You can too.

—Chonda Pierce, recording artist, author, comedian

Leadership in a chaotic world should come with a warning label attached: lead
at your own risk. Leadership can destroy good people, or it can be the singular
challenge that brings them to responsible maturity. Nina Gunter and Gay
Leonard have given us wisdom for the crucible of leadership. It is experience-
tested, Bible-based, and practical. Read this book.

—Dan Boone, president, Trevecca Nazarene University

If there's ever been a world that is hectic, it's ours. If there's ever been a time
where leadership needed to be holy, it's now.

—Mark Rutland, president, Oral Roberts University

Every hectic, harried, hurried, and haggard leader needs to stop long enough
to engage the Spirit in everyday leadership roles. *Holy Leadership in a Hectic
World* encourages us all that we can lead righteously in spite of and during
demanding schedules. Take time for this book. Your followers will thank you.

—Stan Toler, pastor, author, speaker

Holy Leadership in a Hectic World is a convincing call for Christian influence
manifested and magnified by the daily infilling of the Holy Spirit. Nina
Gunter and Gay Leonard testify from personal experience to the difference
leading from a Wesleyan-Holiness perspective makes, as they challenge us
to offer God not just intellect, training, and charisma but a fully-consecrated
life as well. This book is for all who want to find and fulfill God's purpose of
leadership authenticated by Christlike living.

—Jerry Pence, general superintendent, The Wesleyan Church

Gunter and Leonard go beyond pat answers to the Answer. Leadership in any
arena must be based on the careful guidance of the indwelling Holy Spirit.
Keeping in step with the Spirit provides good footprints for others to follow.
Holy Leadership in a Hectic World is a good place to start!

—J. K. Warrick, general superintendent, Church of the Nazarene

Holy Leadership in a Hectic World provides a fresh look at leadership through the lens of holiness. This is a thoughtful and reflective book that also provides relevant and practical points of application—particularly for one who seeks to be a holy leader. Leadership is a daily discipline, a lifelong pursuit, and this fine work will be helpful to leaders in all walks of life and at any point of their leadership journey. I recommend it enthusiastically!

—John C. Bowling, president, Olivet Nazarene University

H O L Y
LEADERSHIP
IN A HECTIC WORLD

BY NINA G. GUNTER
& GAY LEONARD

BEACON HILL PRESS
OF KANSAS CITY

Copyright 2009
by Nina G. Gunter, Gay Leonard,
and Beacon Hill Press of Kansas City

ISBN 978-0-8341-2442-4

Printed in the United States of America

Cover Design: Darlene Filley
Interior Design: Sharon Page

Library of Congress Cataloging-in-Publication Data
Gunter, Nina G.
  Holy Leadership in a hectic world / Nina G. Gunter and Gay Leonard.
    p. cm.
  Includes bibliographical references.
  ISBN 978-0-8341-2442-4 (pbk.)
  1. Leadership—Religious aspects—Christianity. I. Leonard, Gay L., 1953- II. Title.
  BV4597.53.L43G87 2009
  253—dc22

                                              2009005554

10 9 8 7 6 5 4 3 2 1

CONTENTS

INTRODUCTION

Almost everyone we know is busy. Our days are filled with people and tasks, the pleasurable and the troublesome, grand opportunities and dutiful responsibilities.

In this hectic world with constant demands and hurried schedules, we've been privileged to be molded by some busy people who have shown us the priority of being before doing. The difference between the to-do list and the to-be list is the difference between the hectic leader and the holy leader.

In the *filled* bookshelves of leadership manuals, is there need for one more? In the *filled* days of leaders, is there time to read one more? Only if we are convinced that the best practices of leadership are incomplete and inadequate without the direction of the Holy Spirt.

You will read in this book aniecdotes from church, education, music, history, literature, sports, entertainment, and politics. We've shared some of our personal experiences; those not otherwise identified are Nina Gunter's. But most of all, you will notice that this leadership book is heavily seasoned with Scripture. Whether on the platform or behind the scenes, holy leaders operate on the guidance of the Spirit and the principles set forth in the Word of God as the quintessential leadership manual.

We pray that in your hectic world, you will shine like stars, lighting the way for those who follow you because of the daily *infilling* of the Holy Spirit, the ultimate Counselor in every leadership motivation, decision, action.

Nina G. Gunter
Gay Leonard

CHAPTER ONE

DIE DAILY

My life is too hectic, too hurried, too harried. It is under-budgeted, over-scheduled, and ultra-obligated.

I'm asked to do too much in too little time with inadequate resources, outdated equipment, and ill-prepared assistants.

My staff is over-rated, under-motivated, self-consumed, uninspired, uncaring, and unaware.

My team is off-balance, off-task, off-schedule, off-budget, and off-target.

My family is out of control, out of patience, directionless, loveless, and lawless.

I've read every leadership book, attended every parenting seminar, completed every personality profile, taken every self-improvement course, done the strengths-finder inventory, and persevered through every church growth conference I can find—yet I still feel inundated, inadequate, imperfect, unsuccessful, and unfollowed.

I desire to be child-molding, character-building, team-motivating, others-centered, Christ-lifting, and self-effaced—yet I find myself repeatedly demanding, berating, correcting, and criticizing.

So why does God continue to call me to be a leader?

This too-hectic, too-hurried, over-challenged life sends people on a constant search, consciously or unconsciously, for a trustworthy person to follow. As a parent, supervisor, teacher, pastor, employee, or friend, you are being followed. By definition, that makes you a leader.

God's answer to this need for someone to follow, and to the great vacuum of qualified candidates to fill it, is not just leaders—but *holy* leaders. The business world, the MBA schools, the leadership conferences, and the world's bookshelves have outlined seven habits, four strategies, nine team tips, and six steps to leading. Yet they all add up to zero without the God factor. Your forum—family, classroom, church, office—plus your humanistic efforts to provide the best-informed leadership possible will never equate the sum of your willingness to die to self plus the Holy Spirit's infilling to empower you to become a holy leader in this hectic world.

Even as we look behind and spot a follower, we often attempt to evade the role of leadership. Despite hundreds of thousands of young people who emulated his every move, Charles Barkley, voted one of the 50 greatest basketball players in NBA history, denied being a role model. He ran television advertisements saying professional athletes were not role models, creating what the official encyclopedia of the NBA admits was a firestorm of protest. Yet whenever a follower tags behind—invited or not—a leader has been designated.

Attempts to dodge leadership sometimes spring from feelings of inadequacy. We measure ourselves against those who have been our leaders. Many who have had faulty leaders say they want no part of being that faulty. And many who have had outstanding leaders say they could never live up to those standards.

Fear of failure or the pressure to be perfect stops many from pursuing the leadership role to which they have been called by God. Perfectionism can be paralyzing. Students plagued by perfectionism pose a gripping challenge for their teachers. These students avoid any task that they are not completely assured they can do to perfection. They procrastinate on any project that threatens lack of perfect accomplishment. They begin projects over and over, scrapping all that had been completed and starting anew whenever the least flaw occurs, whether it be a single missed note in a piano concerto or merely a stray stroke of penmanship.

Perfectionism plagues marriages. One mate places high expectations on the other, and the relationship cannot bear the weight. Or, some mates set such perfect standards for themselves that they constantly feel they have failed and are therefore unworthy to love or be loved, making it seem impossible to continue the marriage. In either case, perfectionism in one person highlights the other's inability to attend to every detail, resulting in frustration for both.

Indeed, perfectionism can be crippling and debilitating in any relationship—parenting, employment, mentoring, education, or friendship. Failure to be perfect results in avoiding leadership roles, flawed leaders disappointing perfectionist followers, perfectionist leaders giving up on flawed followers.

So why, then, are we, as children of God, admonished to be perfect?

Isn't this against all conventional wisdom? If we as leaders expect ourselves to be perfect, do we not set ourselves up for failure? If we expect those around us to be perfect, do we not frustrate them to the point of avoidance?

God tells us in His Word that He is perfect. We accept His ability to be perfect; after all, He is God.

> He is the Rock, his works are perfect, and all his ways are just. A faithful God who does no wrong, upright and just is he *(Deuteronomy 32:4)*.

> O Lord, you are my God; I will exalt you and praise your name, for in perfect faithfulness you have done marvelous things, things planned long ago *(Isaiah 25:1)*.

> The law of the LORD is perfect, reviving the soul. The statutes of the LORD are trustworthy, making wise the simple *(Psalm 19:7)*.

However, God's Word also tells us that He makes *us* perfect: "It is God who arms me with strength and makes my way perfect" (Psalm18:32).

We have problems when we read God's Word instructing us to be perfect: "Be perfect, therefore, as your heavenly Father is perfect" (Matthew 5:48).

Can people be perfect? It seems impossible. But, if God's Word is reliable, and if He will equip us to do whatever He calls us to do, it is possible for us to be perfect. There are many examples of this throughout the Bible. For example, God looked throughout His world and found the earth corrupt and full of violence, yet He found Noah: "Noah was a just man and perfect in his generations, and Noah walked with God" (Genesis 6:9, KJV). Not only was the command given by Jesus himself in the Sermon on the Mount (Matthew 5:48), but He also prayed in His High-priestly prayer that God would envelop us into the perfect unity that He and His Father and the Holy Spirit enjoyed within the Trinity:

> And the glory which You gave Me I have given them, that they may be one just as We are one: I in them, and You in Me; that they may be made perfect in one, and that the world may know that You have sent Me, and have loved them as You have loved Me *(John 17:22-23, NKJV)*.

Even Paul preached to early Christians to be perfect:

> We proclaim him, admonishing and teaching everyone with all wisdom, so that we may present everyone perfect in Christ *(Colossians 1:28)*.

All of these sound like impossible commands that could not possibly be fulfilled by mere human beings like you and me. But, isn't this in itself a justifiable "out" for being a leader?

Was God trying to saddle us with goals we could not possibly attain? Was Jesus teaching a philosophy not humanly achievable? Did Paul fall prey to establishing more layers of legalism, the very thing he preached against? By no means!

Why, then, does some form of the word *perfect* appear more than a hundred times in Scripture? And why are we called to perfect love? John Wesley, considered the father of Methodism and the Wesleyan-Armenian tradition, said, "I would not use the term, except Paul used it and Jesus used it." But what does it mean?

True, these commandments to be perfect seem encumbering and impossible. But they were not given to point us to failure or to lead others with unattainable standards that would eternally frustrate them and inevitably cause them to fail. On the contrary, the doctrine of Christian perfection given to us by God himself points us toward His grace.

In the same way, it is not my own striving, my performance or lack of performance, my knowledge or lack of knowledge, my ability or lack of ability, that makes me able to fulfill Christ's command to be perfect. It is His grace in me:

> But he said to me, "My grace is sufficient for you, for my power is made perfect in weakness." Therefore I will boast all the more gladly about my weaknesses, so that Christ's power may rest on me *(2 Corinthians 12:9)*.

What does Jesus mean when He issues the formidable command "You shall be perfect"? Our modern definition of the word *perfect* only frustrates our understanding and sends us running in the opposite direction when the world asks for holy leaders to line up. *Perfect*, according to *Merriam-Webster's Dictionary*, means "being entirely without fault or defect." It comes from the Latin word *perfectus*, which means *complete* and *finished* or *fulfilled*, as in "all steps completed, all details finished, case closed." Modern meanings of *perfect* lead us to synonyms like *flawless*, *accurate*, *expert*, *whole*, and *entire*. Which of us can add these accolades to our résumé today or our epitaph tomorrow?

I have several pens. One costs about ninety-five cents at the office supply store. Another is an expensive Montblanc pen, given to me as a gift. Regardless of their costs, writing is the purpose for which both were made. Regardless of their costs, both have the potential to write well, and both have the potential for flaws—streaking, skipping, and leaking. Regardless of the cost, I want the perfect one—the one that fulfills its purpose.

A five-year-old child can be a perfect child if he or she accomplishes what a typical five-year-old can do. Never mind that the child cannot solve a calculus problem, drive a car, or even sit perfectly still for 15 minutes. If he or she is a complete five-year-old capable of the cognitive abilities, motor skills, emotional well-being, physical health, and development of a five-year-old, the doctor will proclaim the child *perfectly* well, able to fulfill the purposes of a child his or her age.

What was the purpose for which God made us? When the Creator God proclaimed to the divine Trinity, "Let us make man in our image, in our likeness" (Genesis 1:26), He did not mean that we would be added to the Trinity. We were not created to *be* God. We were created to be *like* God—in His image, emulating His character and personality.

Unfortunately many have confused the two. Some teachers, parents, employers, ministers, and church laypeople make one of two mistakes: Some avoid their call to leadership, thinking they cannot be perfect like God. Others, taking the full reins of leadership, assume they were created to *be* God—the general manager of the universe and the specific manager of their own little empires.

But the writer of Ephesians tells us our true purpose:

You were taught, with regard to your former way of life, to put off your old self, which is being corrupted by its deceitful desires; to be made new in the attitude of your minds;

and to put on the new self, created to be like God in true
righteousness and holiness *(4:22-24)*.

The purpose for which God made you and me is to be like Him
in true righteousness and holiness. As a new creation in Christ,
we take on His attributes intended as the original purpose of our
first parents. Here it is again, this time from a different version:

Since, then, we do not have the excuse of ignorance,
everything—and I do mean everything—connected with
that old way of life has to go. It's rotten through and
through. Get rid of it! And then take on an entirely new way
of life—a God-fashioned life, a life renewed from the inside
and working itself into your conduct as God accurately reproduces his character in you *(Ephesians 4:22-24, TM)*.

As we fulfill our purpose to be like God, as He "accurately
reproduces his character" (v. 24, TM) in us for roles of holy leadership, we look for His characteristics revealed in His creation,
His Word, His Son, and His Holy Spirit. His creation displays
His unity, organization, and compassion for all living things. His
Word tells us God is love and that He longs to forgive us. His
Son tells us He came to serve, not to be served, and to give His
life as a ransom for many. His Holy Spirit convicts and convinc-
es us of sin and anything unlike God in our character.

We enter upon Christian perfection not when we do everything flawlessly but when we focus all our efforts on loving as
God loves, forgiving as He forgives, and serving as He served.
John Wesley defined perfect love as loving God with your whole
heart, soul, strength, and mind, and loving your neighbor as

yourself (see Luke 10:27). This is the essence of holy living. And being before doing is the essence of holy leadership.

Holiness is not just a doctrine, although it appears in the articles of faith of many denominations. Holiness is more than a sermon topic, although we have heard it preached from many pulpits. Holiness is most of all a lifestyle. It is an experience to be lived rather than merely a theology to be taught. It is an application of grace that we understand best when modeled in the daily actions and words of godly people. It is best believed when seen in the lives of those to whom we look for leadership. It is best taught to others in our being as well as our doing.

Though not perfect in the worldly sense of *flawless*, we can through the grace of God be delivered from the power of rebellion against God. The cleansing, claiming power of the Holy Spirit indwells us, allowing us to be a living application of grace to all who watch and follow our lives.

With the infilling of the Holy Spirit, we have a new hunger and thirst after righteousness. Phineas Bresee, a Holiness preacher in the late 19th and early 20th centuries, said, "A sanctified [holy] life is a delight to Jesus, a joy to the soul, a benediction to the home, a power in the church, a terror to sin, and a continual disappointment to the devil." In the home, in the church, and in the world, a holy life is the shining example of fulfilling the purpose for which we were created.

Holiness is distinguishing; it sets us apart from the world's other leaders. It gives us a new identity and a new commitment to fulfilling our God-created purpose. It enlivens us to a new spiritual level of love and obedience to God that spills over into every aspect of our lives. Leaders with this kind of holy power attract people to a lifestyle where righteousness, justice, and servanthood supersede the bottom line.

I remember coming to that experience in my life. At 14 years of age, I sat in a camp meeting on a hot summer Sunday afternoon. The South Carolina open-air tabernacle floor was covered with sawdust where children played in the sweltering heat. But I ignored the heat, the distractions of the children, and the peer pressure of the other teenagers nearby. Even as a young girl, I was aware of a need in my life. I heard the voice of the Holy Spirit calling me to a full cleansing and filling. Because I was already a believer, had been forgiven of my sins, and was a child of God, I had no rebellion in my heart. I wanted only all that God had for me. I pushed myself away from the friends with whom I sat, walked down to the altar, and said a great big eternal yes to God. That afternoon I died to myself, consecrated myself to God, and received the fullness of His Holy Spirit. My life of leadership has never been the same.

I learned the upside-down economy of God. To be first, we must be last. To be the greatest, we must be the least. And to live fully, we must die. Paul said it best when he wrote, "I have been crucified with Christ and I no longer live, but Christ lives in me" (Galatians 2:20).

In the same way that Christ surrendered himself to the Cross, so we surrender ourselves—die to ourselves—in allowing God full reign over us. Through His death and resurrection, "the righteous requirement of the law might be fulfilled in us who do not walk according to the flesh but according to the Spirit" (Romans 8:4, NKJV). No longer lord over our lives, we allow God himself to take the reign and the throne. We defer to Him for authority, rule, guidance, and decisions. As we walk according to the Spirit, our footsteps are more reliable for others to follow. A holy leader is more emboldened to say, "Follow me as I follow Christ," for the credibility of a Christ-follower attracts more followers.

Since that afternoon when I said the great big yes to God to allow Him to live and myself to die, I have said a lot of little yeses to Him throughout life. Like Paul, who said, "I die every day" (1 Corinthians 15:31), daily I take myself off the throne of my life, consecrate myself to Him, and ask for His Spirit to have control of my life. A life controlled by the Holy Spirit means we have our minds set daily on what the Spirit desires. As the Spirit of God lives in us, our minds, under His daily control, lead to a life of peace (Romans 8:5-6). Only then, in this over-rushed, me-first, hectic society, are we prepared to live in such a way that we should be willing to ask—or even allow—others to follow us. Without the Spirit of God as Lord over every aspect of our daily lives, how can we dare to be lords [leaders] over others?

As we continue to die daily, we remain pure, but only as the Holy Spirit—moment by moment—continues to transform us more and more into the likeness of Jesus Christ. As He cleanses and corrects us, we reflect His character, we take on His traits, we model His lifestyle. We live to fulfill the purpose for which we were created—a perfect, though not flawless, accomplishment of leading others.

Christ's life showed me how, and enabled me to do it. I identified myself completely with him. Indeed, I have been crucified with Christ. My ego is no longer central. It is no longer important that I appear righteous before you or have your good opinion, and I am no longer driven to impress

God. Christ lives in me. The life you see me living is not "mine," but it is lived by faith in the Son of God, who loved me and gave himself for me *(Galatians 2:20, TM).*

In 1984 one of television's most popular commercials aired. Three women examined an enormous hamburger bun with a miniscule meat patty inside. Two of the women were enamored with the size and fluffiness of the bun, but the third, played by actress Clara Peller, gruffly demanded, "Where's the beef?" The commercial earned her a place in television advertising history, and the phrase earned itself a place in American and Canadian vernacular. Apart from the commercial, applied to any topic of conversation, the phrase came to mean, "Where's the real substance of what you claim?" In the 1984 United States presidential primary campaign debates, in response to Gary Hart's perpetual promise of new ideas, Walter Mondale ridiculed, "When I hear your new ideas, I'm reminded of that ad, 'Where's the beef?'"[1]

Followers deserve to ask of their leaders, "Where's the beef in your life?" And when we purport to be holy leaders, we are subject to search not only from our followers and peers but also from God himself: What is the substance of our leadership? Is it humanistic, clever, seminar-gleaned? Or does it ring true with the substance enabled and empowered by the Holy Spirit?

When we surrender ourselves to the lordship of Jesus Christ, we give Him permission to lay claim to all there is of us. When a committee of ministers in England discussed inviting D. L. Moody to serve as the evangelist of a citywide evangelistic campaign, one minister objected, "Why Moody? Does he have a monopoly on the Holy Spirit?" After silence, one minister responded, "No, but the Holy Spirit has a monopoly on Mr. Moody."

Holy leaders share a common characteristic—death. But it is not a death *of* self; it is a death *to* self—their personal desires, passions, and selfish wishes. As the writer of Galatians expressed, "Those who belong to Christ Jesus have crucified the sinful nature with its passions and desires" (5:24).

But there is good news to follow. After death comes resurrection. Spirit-filled leaders still have their unique God-given personalities. Wholly consecrated to God, holy leaders surrender their personalities, temperaments, and dispositions to the Holy Spirit. We submit to the work of the Holy Spirit to help us in our weak areas so that in all we do and say, we become more like Jesus Christ, who said to the Father, "your kingdom come, your will be done" (Matthew 6:10).

The perpetual death to self and resurrection to His rule provide godly "love, joy, peace, patience, kindness, goodness, faithfulness, gentleness and self-control" (Galatians 5:22-23). It is not what *we* can do but what *God* does through us as a work of grace as we are transformed into His image. What follower does not want that kind of leader?

So does God's Spirit create us to be the perfect leader?

Agnes Goxha Bojaxhiu was a simple Albanian peasant girl when she left her homeland at age 18 to devote herself entirely to the calling of God, eventually becoming a nun and teaching school in India. The Spirit drew her heart to suffering and poverty-stricken people, and in 1948 she left the convent for the streets of Calcutta. Without funds or support, she began an open-air school for the slum children found among the poorest of the poor. She loved the dying with such a perfect love that the remainder of her life was devoted to bringing comfort to those who could give nothing in return. That kind of love drew people to come alongside. Unwittingly, she had become a holy leader, and, as financial support and volunteers joined her, the world eventually awarded her the Nobel Peace Prize. The diminutive nun, Mother Teresa, who saw herself only as a simple servant of God, became a great leader—a holy leader—leaving a legacy of followers in the order of the Missionaries of Charity and indirectly in Christians throughout the world.

But was she the perfect leader? After her death, correspondence to her confessor revealed her dark night of the soul, a spiritual emptiness, doubt, and loneliness. "Jesus has a very special love for you. As for me, the silence and the emptiness are so great that I look and do not see, listen and do not hear."[2] Was the perfect holy leader a fraud?

Teleos reminds us that perfection is bringing to completion and fulfilling the purpose for which we were made. Mother Teresa found her purpose humbly. Humility is not so much thinking less of yourself as it is thinking of yourself less. As she said, "We can do no great things, only small things with great love." Throughout her darkness and depression, though she strained to hear the voice of God and found it silent, she never ceased serving Him with the same intensity. In this way, she fulfilled the purpose for which she was created by Almighty God.

Augustine said, "Do you wish to be great? Then begin by being. Do you desire to construct a vast and lofty fabric? Think first about the foundations of humility. The higher your structure is to be, the deeper must be its foundation. . . . Do you wish to rise? Begin by descending. You plan a tower that will pierce the clouds? Lay first the foundation of humility."

Our hectic world is looking for Spirit-filled, humble, holy leaders who will model, guide, and mentor others to be more and more like God. Can we be perfect leaders? Only when we fulfill our purpose. And that job title is open to all of us who are walking in the Spirit, dying one day at a time.

CHAPTER TWO

HEAR YOUR CALLING

J. I. Packer, theologian and author named by TIME magazine as one of "The 25 Most Influential Evangelicals in America" said, "The high spots of my life present themselves in retrospect as a series of surprises—happy surprises, from the hand of a very gracious God."[1] Life brings the unanticipated to all of us—sometimes it's happy; sometimes it's not. Surprises packaged in a very few words have the capability of thrusting us into life-changing roles of leadership:

- You're hired.
- I just need someone to talk to.
- It's a boy.
- The church board would like to consider you to be their new pastor.
- We have a position in another city for which we think you'd fit perfectly.
- I do.

Almost instantaneously we are invited, ushered, or even sucked into a leadership role. But the question is never *Am I a leader?* By virtue of relationships, we all are leaders—to children and aging parents, to friends and peers, to church members and new converts, to employees and clients, to pupils and fellow educators.

The real question is *Am I serving God as a holy leader in the relationships He has given me?* Am I representing Him in all decisions, meetings, and conversations? Am I upholding His values, plans, and character? Am I conducting myself through His power, His wisdom, and His leadership? Am I filtering all I know of the good, secular, leadership principles and practices I have learned about parenting, ministering, educating, and leading through the guidance of His Holy Spirit?

The leadership call from human lips that sometimes comes as a happy surprise must be preceded by a higher calling. For all Spirit-filled Christians, there are spiritual issues to be settled as the foundation for the unanticipated thrown at us by our hectic, over-scheduled, sleep-deprived world. We must first settle the bedrock decision on which all other leadership decisions will be based: *Am I willing to submit myself to becoming a holy leader?*

If we are forgiven believers, walking in the Spirit and living in consecration to His total will, we are all candidates to be holy leaders. We must hear and accept God's calling to holy leadership so that we are prepared at a moment's notice and equipped by His power for unanticipated human interventions that plunge us into holy leadership as a friend, parent, teacher, minister, or leader in any arena.

Am I willing to be called to holy leadership? Am I hearing my calling? Am I accepting that call?

If we live in close proximity to His voice, God will never have to say, *Can you hear me now?*

The word *calling* is best known today as a vocation or profession, especially if it is directed by a strong inner sense of duty accompanied by a conviction of divine instruction. *Call* traces its roots to the English language before the 12th century. It comes from Old Norse *kalla*, similar to Old English hilde*calla*, which was a battle herald. From the battle cry similarities, c*all* came to mean speaking in a loud voice, such as calling the troops to fall out or calling the family to dinner, but its implications spread into metaphors like tributaries of a river.[2]

Take, for instance, the toss of a coin on the football field. The referee asks the players to "call the toss"—heads or tails. It seems a matter of total luck; nothing more than a guess. Yet *call*'s cousin word, interestingly, is *predict*—literally to say before, "to declare or indicate in advance."[3] If football players could truly predict supernaturally, they would have the advantage in making the call every time. But only One can do that. The calling we experience as Christians comes not by chance but through One who is always and forever omniscient. Our calling is from the divine God.

Acceptance of the call to holy leadership from an omniscient God provides the foundation for the specific opportunities to lead. Even holy leaders must recognize that not every job offer is a call of God. If it were, some of us would be moving our families from city to city every six months.

When the commitment has been settled to follow God in every decision as a holy leader rather than a climb-the-ladder, seek-the-promotion, get-the-glory leader, we can eagerly seek His will for specific circumstances. Each role must be confirmed first by God himself, rather than by the intervention of human beings. It is God who calls, not the church or the school or the boss. Human callings must always be subjected to the divine litmus test: "Dear friends, do not believe every spirit, but test the spirits to see whether they are from God" (1 John 4:1).

In fact, specific leadership offers sometimes take our focus off the divine call. Employment offers or new relationships or lay leadership church elections sometimes derail us from the foundation: Are we seeking new platforms for power, or are we continually submitting ourselves to His power? Are we called, and are we *being* called in daily surrender?

God speaks in such a way that if we are truly the sheep of His pasture, we know it is Him. If we are connected to the Good Shepherd, we recognize His voice and have no fear in following Him, regardless how daunting the task, how limited our resources, or how humanly enticing—or unenticing—the offer. We follow His calling to holy leadership when we know Him. As it says in the Gospel of John, "He calls his own sheep by name and leads them out. When he has brought out all his own, he goes on ahead of them, and his sheep follow him because they know his voice" (10:3-4). There is great comfort in knowing—

- **God knows who you are.** Before time began or the earth was formed, before you were born or even conceived, God knew you. He created you to be the leader He is calling you to be.
- **God knows where you are.** He understands the conditions under which you live; your geographical, economic, or spiritual struggles; the emotional baggage you carry. He has a plan for where you are to stay or the path toward new territory He has for you to discover. He knows

the context out of which He is calling you to be His holy leader.

- **God knows your abilities.** He knows your unholy pride in your accomplishments and your arrogance in the strengths He gave you. He understands the limitations you feel, the weaknesses that plague you, the obstacles that seem insurmountable. He knows the unlimited opportunities He is offering to you.

The great spiritual irony is that to this God who calls us, woos us, and waits eagerly for us to respond to Him, the majority of our prayers often are centered on asking Him to attend to *our* calling. To the Creator of the universe who—though He needs nothing to make himself complete—asks for our hands, our feet, our voices, and our hearts to work through in order to lead others, we respond by asking Him to answer our requests, come to our aid, and care for our problems. We are more concerned that He hears our voices than that we hear His voice.

Answer me when I call to you, O my righteous God. Give me relief from my distress; be merciful to me and hear my prayer *(Psalm 4:1)*.

Hear my voice when I call, O Lord; be merciful to me and answer me *(Psalm 27:7)*.

Hear me, O God, as I voice my complaint; protect my life from the threat of the enemy *(Psalm 64:1)*.

The psalmist's litany goes on and on. His petitions appear to be all about his needs, his wants, and his seeming impatience to receive immediate responses for help and triumph over others. But before we judge, we must consider our own prayer life.

How interested are we in waiting quietly, listening rather than speaking, obeying rather than supplicating? How guilty are we in seeking authority and reigning over others? How eager are we to be *holy* leaders, submitted to where God has placed us and the role He has given us? How earnest are we about hearing our calling? And, when we remember who is calling, in the midst of our striving, whining, and questioning, we must say, like Job, "I am unworthy—how can I reply to you? I put my hand over my mouth" (40:4). As Patsy Clairmont, "Women of Faith" speaker and author, says, "Some of us will need both hands."

God's call is not generic. Though it is for all, it is not en masse. God knows you; He knows the leadership role on which He has carved your personal initials, and He calls you by name. Regardless of how long ago, most believers can remember details about the first time God called them by name to come to Him for forgiveness of sin. For many, the voice inside pounded their hearts like the pulsating thrust of the Space Shuttle launching from its pad. For others, it was a still, quiet voice. Powerfully or peacefully, He said to each of us, as He, the Lord of hosts, said specifically to His chosen people, "Return to me, and I will return to you" (Malachi 3:7). We recall after confession and repentance the great release from the pain and heaviness of sin. For some, it seemed as though a thousand angels sang audibly! Though Christ died for many, His death was individual for each of us. He called us personally to salvation.

As we remember our conversion experiences, individual to each of us, we can understand that in the same way He calls us personally to holy leadership. If the reward of accepting this calling is no less exhilarating than His forgiveness of sin, why, then, do we resist?

In 1955, during an era when the American South was characterized by racial segregation, Rosa Parks refused to give up her bus seat to a white person in Montgomery, Alabama. Though this simple act launched the Civil Rights Movement, it floundered for lack of leadership. To fill that void, a local Baptist pastor from Atlanta, just 26 years old at the time, stepped in to oversee the boycott of Montgomery's segregated bus system. The Civil Rights Movement had found its leader—Martin Luther King Jr. Through peaceful resistance, demonstrations, and marches, he inspired people with hope that their world could be different. The movement culminated in one of the most strategic turning points in American history in 1963 as King led a nonviolent march to Washington, D.C. There, at the Lincoln Memorial, he addressed a quarter of a million people with one of the best-known speeches in history.

Yet Martin Luther King Jr. was a reluctant leader. On the 40th anniversary of his assassination, Andrew Young, civil rights activist who was with King on the day of his death, remarked, "Martin was very authentic. He was for real. *He didn't want to be a leader.*"[4]

How many times have we told our children that pursuing dreams that we consider to be the only path to happiness will pale ludicrously when we accept God's Plan A? Yet each of us must learn on his or her own, turning from rebellion to submission, from reluctant leader to the personal acceptance of His calling, and look back with chagrin on the insignificance of self-inspired plans. When we look at the assurance from the prophet Jeremiah, we find that God does indeed have a plan:

Yes. Believe it or not, this is the Message from God-of-the-Angel-Armies . . . "I'll show up and take care of you as I promised and bring you back home. I know what I'm doing. I have it all planned out—plans to take care of you, not abandon you, plans to give you the future you hope for. When you call on me, when you come and pray to me, I'll listen. When you come looking for me, you'll find me . . . I'll make sure you won't be disappointed" (*Jeremiah 29:8, 10-14, TM*).

Many of the corporate world's popular leadership principles promote teamwork, all the while factoring in opportunities for personal promotions, bonuses, and corporate perks. Even books on servant leadership refer to achieving results by cultivating relationships, managing with compassion, helping others achieve their goals, and benefiting the entire unit over self. Some of these resources mention the original Servant Leader, who took the towel and stooped from divinity to wash the feet of His followers.

In this get-ahead, me-first world, God is not searching for corporate gurus, employees of the month, perfect parents, or teachers of the year. Anyone who seeks to lead without a divine call or enabling will receive his or her reward in full in this life—and it will be an endless cycle of chasing ambition, achieving at best only a fleeting version of success. As 17th-century English clergyman and scholar Robert Burton said, "Like dogs in a wheel, birds in a cage, or squirrels in a chain, ambitious men still climb and climb, with great labor and incessant anxiety but never reach the top."

Ambition, dreams, beliefs, determination—these are leadership qualities that, in human hands, may become manipulative; but, surrendered to the Spirit by dying daily to self, they can become consecrated tools. In God's reverse-to-earth values, where the greatest is the least and the first is the last, the calling for holy leaders originates with God himself. Paul listed all his credentials: circumcised on the eighth day, descended from the tribe of Benjamin, a Hebrew among Hebrews, a Pharisee, full of zeal (see Philippians 3:5-6). Yet over and over, Paul identifies himself as an apostle—not by his lineage, by his own merit or choosing, or by the appointment of any other human being—"by the will of God" only (1 Corinthians 1:1; 2 Corinthians 1:1; Ephesians 1:1; Colossians 1:1; 2 Timothy 1:1). Even Jesus Christ himself was appointed High Priest by His Father.

> No one takes this honor upon himself; he must be called by God, just as Aaron was. So Christ also did not take upon himself the glory of becoming a high priest. But God said to him, "You are my Son; today I have become your Father" *(Hebrews 5:4-5)*.

What happens when God calls your name to be a holy leader?

For me, the calling came in the summer of 1950 as I visited my sister and her husband when they were students at Trevecca Nazarene College (now University). Only 12 years of age, I was sitting alone in their little apartment while they were gone to class and having my morning quiet time with God. I had been sensing that God was talking to me about a special calling, but I had not yet discovered what it was. That morning, my earnestness to love God and seek His will rose above my young age, and I agonized in prayer. I remember it as vividly as if it were today. In seeking His voice, I did something I almost never do: I let my Bible fall open indiscriminately as I searched for divine guidance. Immediately my eyes fell on 1 Samuel 2:18: "Samuel was ministering before the Lord—a boy wearing a linen ephod." Did these words refer to my youthfulness? Later in life I learned that my name, Nina, means "little girl." When I read that scripture in 1 Samuel, I had the assurance that He was confirming His calling of a 12-year-old girl to preach. The warmth of God's confirmation and peace flooded my soul, and I have never doubted God's call from that moment on.

God calls preachers and nurses and counselors and bankers. He calls us as volunteers to teach Sunday School and sing in the choir and work with the youth and serve on the board. These are the arms of His calling. But God first calls us to holy leadership.

What happens when God calls you to be His holy leader? Saul was struck blind and fell to the ground. James and John left their nets immediately. Mary was startled out of her grief and sent running with the news of the Resurrection. The reactions are as individual as His calling, but timeless principles remain from the God who is the same yesterday, today, and forever.

When God calls your name, He gets your attention. Moses, the great liberating leader of the Hebrews, was first attracted to God by the supernatural. Moses was intrigued, curious, and incredulous that a bush—obviously on fire—was not burned up. But the call was not in the bush. The call was from the God of the fire, who said personally to him, "Moses, Moses!" (Exodus 3:4).

When God calls your name, He gives you a personal invitation. He invited Moses to a place that many long for but few invest effort to find—holy ground. Moses accepted the invitation and removed his sandals. He hid his face, fearful to look at the Almighty God but reveled in the holy presence from which he could not hide.

When God calls your name, He identifies himself. Before Moses could even voice the inquiry, God said, "I am the God of your father, the God of Abraham, the God of Isaac and the God of Jacob" (Exodus 3:6). God's voice is definable and recognizable. He does not speak in riddles or play games to see if, in our finite humanity, we can catch on. He speaks like no other spirit or human being.

When God calls your name, He commissions you for divine assignment. God recounted to Moses His awareness of the plight of His people. Under the oppressing hand of slavery, their cry had reached omniscient ears. "So, now, go," said God. "I am sending you" (Exodus 3:10).

God's calling is a summons. Like the official document issued by the court legally mandating our presence at a set time and in a set place, God's summons is official, authoritarian, specific, and expectant. To disobey His summons is to suffer the consequences—not of the wrath of God but of the missed opportunities for a life of fulfillment, happiness, and deliverance for ourselves and for those we are called to lead.

Louise Chapman, a great mentor in my life, once said to me, "Always remember you are under assignment from God. You are where you are because God put you there and needs you there." The assignment is not ours; the location is not of our choosing. The sovereign God summons individual leaders to specific assignments in unique settings for ultimate purposes at just the right time.

When God calls your name, He guarantees His resources. Moses doubted and debated. *God, are you sure you can pull this* *off? God, do you realize who Pharaoh is? Do you remember my many weaknesses? I have no credibility with the people. They'll ask me who sent me, and when I tell them, they won't believe me anyway. I'm the poorest spokesman you could have chosen. My words come slowly and awkwardly. This will never work. I'm not important enough!*

Our own judgment of importance is irrelevant to God. Our calling is not about how esteemed or eloquent or gifted we are. Our calling is all about the One who calls—His importance, His wisdom, His Word, His unlimited power. All the riches of His authority and abundance are at the disposal of those who accept His calling.

Our location is irrelevant to God. Our calling is not about where we are. It is about the One who will go with us to where He is sending us.

What would Moses do today? How would he respond to the burning-bush, take-off-your-sandals, I-AM call of God? How would our hectic, fast-paced, high-octane world respond to Him?

To Moses' guilty plea of ignorance, our self-help world would say,

If you want to be a leader, read more books, go back to school, search deep for the little god within yourself, take pointers from the leadership gurus, model yourself after corporate giants. All this will overcome your lack of education and experience, Moses. Just study harder.

But to those God is calling to leadership, He says, just as He said to Moses, "I AM WHO I AM. This is what you are to say to the Israelites: 'I AM has sent me to you'" (Exodus 3:14). The Great I AM says, *I will teach you.*

Our fix-it-fast, corporate-structured world would say, If you do not know how to handle it, call a committee together, appoint a think tank, form a focus group, set a meeting.

Every leader eventually has to work with committees and boards. When we pool our knowledge, we have a deeper source from which to drink. A good leader must know how to cast vision, establish teamwork, and gain synergy from combined talents.

But this is not our source of wisdom. God says to those He is calling to leadership, "If any of you lacks wisdom, he should ask God, who gives generously to all without finding fault, and it will be given to him" (James 1:5). When the leadership task is perplexing, we go to the God who not only gives wisdom; by His very character, He *is* wisdom.

To Moses' guilty plea of doubt, our impatient, over-confident world would say, If you don't think people will follow you, work on being more self-assertive. Believe in yourself and others will believe in you. Build your confidence, listen to motivation tapes, adopt a more charismatic persona, Moses. Just get a grip.

God says to those He is calling to leadership, *I am who I say I am, and I can do what I say I can do.*

God is capable of extreme object lessons. To Moses, He turned a rod into a snake and restored it into a rod. He turned a clean hand into a leprous one and restored it to perfect health. Yet even in the middle of God's miraculous display of power available to him, Moses ran from the rod-turned-snake. The awe-inspiring power of His Holy Spirit is given to enable us, yet we continue to doubt even as God is displaying His omnipotence for our eyes only. At the very moment He offers divine resources, we are sometimes crouching, fearfully asking, *Can anything good happen here?*

> If you don't know what you're doing, pray to the Father. He loves to help. You'll get his help, and won't be condescended to when you ask for it. Ask boldly, believingly, without a second thought. People who "worry their prayers" are like wind-whipped waves. Don't think you're going to get anything from the Master that way, adrift at sea, keeping all your options open *(James 1:5-7, TM)*.

To Moses' guilty plea of inability, our self-help world would say, If you don't think you're sufficiently able, take a public speaking course. get some experience. Believe so completely in what you have to say that your confidence will overcome your inabilities, Moses. Just practice a little. But God says to those He is calling to leadership, *When you can't, I can. When you are weak, I am strong. Through my Holy Spirit I will sharpen your skills and make you capable for the task to which I have called you.*

> But he said to me, "My grace is sufficient for you, for my power is made perfect in weakness." Therefore I will boast all the more gladly about my weaknesses, so that Christ's power may rest on me. That is why, for Christ's sake, I delight in weaknesses, in insults, in hardships, in persecutions, in difficulties. For when I am weak, then I am strong *(2 Corinthians 12:9-10)*.

If we could accomplish within ourselves all He has called us to do, why would we need God? His call may move us out of our comfort zone but not away from His presence and power. God promises us, as He did Moses: "My Presence will go with you, and I will give you rest" (Exodus 33:14).

God expects us to work hard, prepare ourselves, and learn all that we can. But only He can give us the spiritual abilities and tools to fulfill God-called leadership roles. God gave Moses the rod and instructed him to use it to do miraculous signs. The rod was a tool, but it was not God. Education, talents, strategies, skills, ideas, and charisma are tools, but they are not God.

When the inevitable time comes when we have no tricks left in our human duffle bag, God will still be there.

> When you come to the end of all the light you know, and it's time to step into the darkness of the unknown, faith is knowing that one of two things shall happen: Either you will be given something solid to stand on or you will be taught to fly.—Edward Teller

Our faith is in the eternal, calling God who has all the resources we need. When we come to the end of our abilities, we must step out into the darkness with assurance, relying not on ourselves but on the God of limitless ability.

God's calling to become a holy leader has nothing to do with who you are, where you have been, who you know, or what you possess. Everything is about the Giver of the calling. Holy leaders lead not of their own abilities but through the daily infilling of His Holy Spirit, who provides all the power needed for us to accomplish His mission:

> All authority in heaven and on earth has been given to me. Therefore go and make disciples of all nations, baptizing them in the name of the Father and of the Son and of the Holy Spirit, and teaching them to obey everything I have commanded you. And surely I am with you always, to the very end of the age *(Matthew 28:18-20).*

To everyone who will hear His calling and accept His mission for holy leadership, He promises He will be known. "Whether you turn to the right or to the left, your ears will hear a voice behind you, saying, 'This is the way; walk in it'" (Isaiah 30:21).

One of the most poignant, iconic photographs of the Martin Luther King Jr. saga is one of his family standing around his open coffin. The photograph is of his wife Coretta and their children, those same four children who were forever immortalized in one of the most quoted speeches in history: "I have a dream that my four little children will one day live in a nation where they will not be judged by the color of their skin but by the content of their character."

The youngest of King's children, Bernice, was only five years old that day, her little head barely peeking over the edge of the casket. Forty years later, on April 4, 2008, in an interview on NBC's *Today*, Ann Curry asked Bernice about her inability to comprehend the events of the fateful day that took her father and of the days to follow that rocked the nation with riots, nonviolent demonstrations, and a national outpouring of grief. It was more than a decade after his death, as she watched a documentary about her father, that Bernice fully embraced the truth and felt the emotional reality for the first time. For two hours, she confesses, she sobbed almost uncontrollably. She lashed out at an unseen enemy, at what could have been, at what never would be. She asked her father why he left her and asked God why He had taken him.

In response to Bernice's confession, Curry asked, "What answers have you gotten to those questions?"

Bernice replied, "My calling to the ministry has greatly answered the question, because I now understand that the sacrifice our father made to change a nation and a world was a part of his calling into ministry. In Christian ministry we believe that you die to yourself so that you might serve humankind."[5]

Rev. Bernice King did not simply follow in her father's footsteps. She did not merely pick up his mantle or take on his occupation by heredity or DNA or inheritance. Rev. King accepted her calling from God. She recognized not her father's voice but her Heavenly Father's voice calling her by name to a specific leadership role.

Happy surprises from the hand of a gracious God? Yes, often. But not all the time. God's calling also comes in the crucible of our suffering and loss. It comes in the loneliness of the barren desert as we are tending sheep. It comes in the awesome voice of the Almighty from the flames of a bush that is not consumed. It comes in the majestic presence of a God so great that, for our own safety, He hides our faces in the cleft of a rock so that we see only the train of His glory as He passes by. It comes in the anointing of oil on the most unlikely little shepherd's head. It comes in the blinding light that knocks us to the ground. It comes in the most precious voice in history, walking alongside the lake where water laps softly against the shore, calling to those of us who are the least significant and educated. It comes in the comforting, revealing voice of the Resurrected One in the garden of our grief, calling our name.

God summons in surprises and sorrows. He calls all kinds of candidates.

So as the Holy Spirit says: "Today, if you hear his voice, do not harden your hearts" (Hebrews 3:7-8).

Can you hear him now?

CHAPTER THREE

CONNECT TO THE POWER SOURCE

Brainstorm a list of the most powerful inanimate objects on earth, and you are likely to visualize some of these natural and man-made sources of power:

- The waters of the Niagara River flowing as far as 167 feet, crashing over giant boulders in a spectacular spray of mist and creating the American and Canadian sections that together comprise the famous Niagara Falls.
- The mushroom cloud rising ominously over Hiroshima after the dropping of "Little Boy," the first nuclear weapon, in 1945.
- The 4.36 million cubic yards of concrete of the Hoover Dam that rises 726.4 feet to hold back the Colorado River.
- The out-of-this-world Hubble Telescope, which, with the aid of the W. M. Keck Telescopes, sends us images of stars, planets, galaxies, and nebulae as far as 13 billion light-years away.

- Hurricane Katrina, believed to be the costliest natural disaster in U. S. history, which killed at least 1,836 people and flooded 80 percent of New Orleans.
- The laser, capable of cutting through steel and titanium, yet whose power can be harnessed to delicately reshape the cornea of the human eye for perfect vision.

In all your brainstorming of powerful icons, however, you are not likely to list The Spruce Goose. For all that Howard Hughes is known for, the embarrassing blight of his biography is that he designed and spearheaded the creation of a wooden "flying boat." In 1942, with the world at war and 800,000 tons of American supplies lost to German submarines, a partnership was formed between Henry Kaiser and Howard Hughes, international oil tycoon, businessman, movie producer, aeronautical engineer, and aviator. The Hughes Kaiser Corporation obtained an $18 million government contract to construct three flying boats to transport troops and supplies across the Atlantic Ocean. The design called for a single-hull flying boat powered by eight 3,000-horsepower engines, wings each 20 feet longer than a football field, and load capacity of 750 troops. After tremendous design and engineering problems, delays, and the eventual desertion of Kaiser, Hughes pursued alone in developing one seaplane. But it was too late and too costly. When the war ended in 1945, the prototype had exceeded the government's funding and still was not completed. Though the plane was constructed of bands of birch, observers derisively dubbed it The Spruce Goose. It took its maiden and only voyage/flight November 2, 1947, flying a little more than one mile at an altitude of 70 feet for approximately one minute. Investigators determined the single cause of its failure: Its low-design cruising speed was almost equivalent to its stall speed. The seaplane was woefully underpowered.[1]

Of all God's attributes—His holiness, His love, His compassion—we see His power displayed from the beginning. The power of His spoken word brought into being what before did not exist: "And God said, 'Let there be light,' and there was light" (Genesis 1:3). Now that's power.

The One who spoke the earth into being as His handiwork and populated the seas with every swimming creature, the skies with every winged bird, the land with every wild animal, livestock, and moving creature, and the world with humankind in His own image did all this through His omnipotence as the Almighty God.

The Trinity displays an orchestrated symphony of power: The Creator God, who ordered the stars and planets and universes beyond our scope of imagination or even the reach of the Hubble; Jesus the Christ, who commanded demons to come out of possessed, caused lame to leap and blind to see, forgave sin, and burst forth from the tomb triumphant over death; the Holy Spirit, who filled, empowered, and transformed a scattered band of ragged deserters into a life-changing, upside-down, world-turning troupe of evangelists. Niagara Falls is but a thimble of water measured on God's scales of omnipotence.

To say that leadership methods and practices today are power-oriented is to say that kids like ice cream. Virtually nothing is higher on the leadership wish list than power. Books, seminars, and speakers all stress the power of influence, the power of team, personal power, and harnessing power. The 1980s brought us the power lunch and the power nap. Red was proclaimed the power color. If you wanted to make a strong impression, get your ideas to stand out in a meeting, manipulate the conversation, and dominate the competition, you wore a red tie. Yes, a red tie would make or break your career. Women donned dark suits and red scarves for the board room. But soon the power tie turned yellow, followed shortly by an article that proclaimed the new power color was pink. No one believed it.

Did the revolving color wheel really make anyone more powerful? Could a tie or scarf really elevate the wearer or bolster his or her mediocre ideas beyond their deserved place? Have we as Christians learned anything about the shallowness of some of secular leadership's "best practices"?

Real power for real holy leadership comes only from the Holy Spirit. "You will receive power when the Holy Spirit comes on you" (Acts 1:8).

Power came into the Middle English language about 1250-1300 through the Anglo-French *poer* and the Vulgar Latin *potēre*, which both meant "to be able." Branches from Latin gave it several nuances of meaning including strength; ability; enablement; having authority over, rule over, or command of. The one used in Acts 1:8 to describe the quality of the Holy Spirit the disciples were promised is *dunamis*. It has two meanings, and from these we get two English words. First, it means strength, from which our English word *dynamite* is derived. Second, it means enablement, capability, and inherent power. From this meaning we get our English word *dynamo*. Like dynamite, the explosive power of the Holy Spirit is able to destroy the strongholds of Satan. Like a dynamo, the Spirit continually produces power, controlling and sustaining the supply, akin to a power plant. We need both the power to face our world as a leader for

Christ today and the promise that the power supply will be there for the challenges of tomorrow.

In order to connect to the proper power source to be equipped as leaders, we must first examine the motives that drive us to seek power.

- Are our motives honorable?
- Are they to further temporal or eternal values?
- Are they of the flesh or of the Spirit?
- Have they been tested against the standards set forth in God's Word?
- Are they consistent with His purposes?
- Are they in keeping with His individual calling for a specific assignment in a God-given leadership role?
- Is our ultimate purpose to accomplish His mission?

If we must honestly respond that our motives and purposes are temporal, fleshly, unbiblical, self-centered, and secular, we can connect only to the power sources of ego, competition, ladder-climbing, and manipulation. Like dynamite, these are tested and explosive methods of achieving power for destructive purposes, which when fueled by an insatiable desire for self-promotion achieve their goals, albeit leaving a string of corpses in their wake. The ways of the world do work for a season; Satan has proven that since the Garden era.

Some of the most powerful figures in human history have subscribed to these methods, proving in deadly ways the maxim that raw power corrupts: Roman Emperor Caligula, so evil he was deemed mad; Roman Emperor Nero, early persecutor of Christians; Adolf Hitler, perpetrator of the Holocaust and other atrocities; Idi Amin, Ugandan dictator known as "Butcher of Africa;" Pol Pot, whose reign of terror over his own Cambodian people lasted almost 35 years and made "The Killing Fields" a globally known phrase—to name just a few.

Some of us could add names of coworkers, bosses, principals, and even pastors who play these roles on a smaller stage but with equal gusto. But just as the news cameras captured the historic photos of Saddam Hussein's statue being toppled from its pedestal, so God himself determines who will have His power to lead.

> He brings princes to naught and reduces the rulers of this world to nothing. No sooner are they planted, no sooner are they sown, no sooner do they take root in the ground, than he blows on them and they wither, and a whirlwind sweeps them away like chaff *(Isaiah 40:23-24)*.

Those who are answering the call to holy leadership must connect to the proper power source. The irony of God's divine plan for fueling holy leadership is that it is most beautifully displayed in those who shun arrogance, ego, and the platform. This kind of power comes to leaders only when we submit ourselves to the Holy Spirit. Given full reign to examine every space of our hearts, He will reveal to us true righteousness and convince us of any unconfessed, unforgiven sin. Jesus said of the promise of the Holy Spirit, who was to come in fullness after the departure of Jesus from this world: "When he [the Holy Spirit] comes, he will convict the world of guilt in regard to sin and righteousness and judgment" (John 16:8).

We Evangelical believers often have a hard time admitting that we have sinned. Though we believe God's Word, that it is possible to live above sin in this life—"My dear children, I write this to you so that you will not sin" (1 John 2:1)—we must go on to embrace the next portion of that Scripture, accepting the fact that continued sin is possible and places us in great need of Christ's atonement:

> But if anybody does sin, we have one who speaks to the Father in our defense—Jesus Christ, the Righteous One. He is the atoning sacrifice for our sins, and not only for ours but also for the sins of the whole world *(1 John 2:1-2)*.

Which of us as leaders has not had a time of regret for words harshly spoken, decisions selfishly made, impatience exhibited, or kindnesses omitted? Those seeking the power to live out God's summons to be holy leaders must subject themselves to the unreserved and continual examination of the Holy Spirit. Are we living in righteousness, managing not only operations but people with justice and compassion? Are we truthful in our conversations? Do we keep our word? Is our reputation in good standing? Do our actions bear out our witness?

Where we fall short or fail miserably in any of these areas, there is a place within Holiness theology for repentance based on the correction of the Holy Spirit. Pastor and author A. W. Tozer painfully put his finger right on the scourge of the Church when he wrote,

> The self-sins . . . dwell too deep within us and are too much a part of our natures to come to our attention till the light of God is focused upon them. The grosser manifestations of these sins—egotism, exhibitionism, self-promotion—are strangely tolerated in Christian leaders, even in circles of impeccable orthodoxy. They are so much in evidence as actually, for many people, to become identified with the gospel. I trust it is not a cynical observation to say that they appear these days to be a requisite for popularity in

some sections of the Church visible. Promoting self under the guise of promoting Christ is currently so common as to excite little notice.

God calls us as leaders to empty ourselves of self and to be sensitive to the conviction and convincing of His Spirit. He gives us grace to repent. As we grow in our knowledge of His nature and His will, and as Satan tempts those closest to God as he did Jesus in the wilderness, we will continue to repent even after we have received Jesus Christ as Lord.

R. T. Williams, general superintendent in the Church of the Nazarene (1916-1946), once severely and publicly reprimanded a pastor who delivered his annual report to convention delegates. It had not been a stellar year for this pastor or his congregation, and Dr. Williams took the opportunity to make him an example of slothful, negligent leadership. When the meeting was dismissed for the noon hour, the Holy Spirit began His turn at reprimanding Dr. Williams for his uncompassionate, unkind leadership. When the business resumed, he began by making a public confession and apology. The Holy Spirit had so convicted and corrected him, he witnessed, that he had fasted lunch and instead prayed for forgiveness and direction throughout the noon hour. He pledged himself as a prayer partner with that struggling pastor and congregation for the next full year, asking God to bring a mighty revival to them, and in faith they would pray that next year's report would reveal the church's greatest year of victory for Christ's sake.

Holy leaders in the power of the Holy Spirit submit themselves to God's correction, to humble repentance, and to one another for accountability.

The Holy Spirit provides a connection to God otherwise impossible. Imagine a great dilemma in your company, your church, or your family. Imagine the heavy weight of responsibility that rests solely with you as the leader. You alone must make the all-important decision: Who will be laid off? Should you sell or hold? How should you punish your child? Who will receive the promotion? Do you pass or fail this student? How much capital should you borrow? How will you handle the discovery of fraud, mismanagement of funds, or interoffice adultery?

Now envision driving to the livestock pen, selecting a bull, swiping your credit card, and loading the animal into a rented trailer. You deliver him to the church, corral him down the center aisle to the altar, and with no small amount of manipulation coax your pastor to join you in flailing away at this animal with knives and swords until he lies blood-splattered, slaughtered, and disemboweled over a large part of the sanctuary. Then you ask God to give you the answer to your dilemma/decision.

Or consider the better way . . .

> Day after day every priest stands and performs his religious duties; again and again he offers the same sacrifices, which can never take away sins. But when this priest [Jesus Christ] had offered for all time one sacrifice for sins, he sat down at the right hand of God . . . by one sacrifice he has made perfect forever those who are being made holy *(Hebrews 10:11-12, 14).*

In this new covenant, the Holy Spirit plays an integral role:

> The Holy Spirit confirms this: This new plan I'm making with Israel isn't going to be written on paper, isn't going to be chiseled in stone; This time "I'm writing out the plan

in them, carving it on the lining of their hearts" *(Hebrews 10:15-16, TM)*.

Without the Holy Spirit to connect us to God, Christianity would be a religion rather than a relationship. Without the Holy Spirit to connect us to God, leaders would be success-driven rather than Spirit-directed.

Through Christ Jesus, we have exchanged bulls and goats for the Perfect Sacrifice, who in turn sent One just like himself, the Comforter and Counselor. He guides us in the normal, day-to-day living out of our Christian faith as leaders in the home, church, and marketplace.

When faced with a difficult decision, according to God's Word we have two options for wisdom. The first is the "wisdom" of this world, which brings its own results:

> Mean-spirited ambition isn't wisdom. Boasting that you are wise isn't wisdom. Twisting the truth to make yourselves sound wise isn't wisdom. It's the furthest thing from wisdom—it's animal cunning, devilish conniving. Whenever you're trying to look better than others or get the better of others, things fall apart and everyone ends up at the others' throats *(James 3:14-16, TM)*.

On the contrary, holy leaders seek true wisdom. If we desire it, we need merely ask the Author of all wisdom:

> If any of you lacks wisdom, he should ask God, who gives generously to all without finding fault, and it will be given to him. But when he asks, he must believe and not doubt, because he who doubts is like a wave of the sea, blown and tossed by the wind *(James 1:5)*.

True wisdom that comes from the counsel of the Holy Spirit also brings its own results:

> But the wisdom that comes from heaven is first of all pure; then peace-loving, considerate, submissive, full of mercy and good fruit, impartial and sincere. Peacemakers who sow in peace raise a harvest of righteousness *(James 3:17-18)*.

In contrast, if we are looking for examples to shun of actions based on bad advice or foolish decisions, the list is long in every arena of life—history, the arts, sports, and entertainment.

- Capitol Records turned down the Beatles four times before finally agreeing to release their records because Jay Livingstone, Capitol's senior executive in New York, did not think the Beatles would have any success in the American market. Seventy-three million viewers who tuned in to see their debut on "The Ed Sullivan Show" in 1964 evidently did not agree.

- The von Trapp family, real-life characters depicted in *The Sound of Music*, saw very little of the profits of the bio-graphic Broadway play or the film (the latter being one of the largest-grossing films in history), because Maria sold the film rights to German producers and inadvertently signed away her rights in the process.

- Scouts for Florida State University football program reported that a high school kid from Monticello, Florida, would never play a single down of Division 1 college football. Jack Youngblood went on to become both a College Hall of Famer at the University of Florida, played in Super Bowl XIV, and was inducted into the National Football League Hall of Fame in Canton, Ohio, in 2001.

Good leaders in all arenas want to make decisions from the best-informed position. They want to strategize based on facts, research, knowledge, and understanding. But holy leaders take a giant step beyond. They make decisions based not merely on the best counsel but on the Counselor, not on truth but on the Truth:

> When he [the Counselor], the Spirit of truth, comes, he will guide you into all truth. He will not speak on his own; he will speak only what he hears, and he will tell you what is yet to come. He will bring glory to me by taking from what is mine and making it known to you *(John 16:13-14)*.

The Holy Spirit has come to transform us into the image of Christ. Jesus was the ultimate leadership model. He called others to follow Him during His time on this earth, and through His Holy Spirit He continues to call holy leaders to follow Him today.

Jesus washed the feet of His disciples to set for us the supreme model of humility and servant leadership. But let's face it—He washed the feet of His disciples because they were dirty. In that day, on the country trails and dusty city roads, disciples literally followed so closely that it is said that disciples "wore" the dust of their master. The clothing and very bodies of Jesus' 12 disciples were physically covered with the dust kicked up by His sandals.

The more closely we follow the Master leadership model, the more thickly we will be covered with the dust of His character. We will wear His humility, His compassion, His kindness, His mercy. Created in His image, marred by sin, we will be transformed—re-formed to our original intent to live and look like Him—by the connection and correction of the Holy Spirit. Without the divine transformation of the infilling of the Holy Spirit, we are simply dirt-encrusted imposters.

God longs to perfect His creation by renewing His purpose in us. In His image, living according to the daily direction of His Spirit, we can lead others with righteousness, justice, and wisdom. He yearns to rid us of self-desire and indulgence, to guide us in the daily crucifixion of self, and to resurrect us in new life like Christ.

Just as an artist signs his creation, and in the same way that the signature increases the value of the artwork, so God desires to imprint His very name upon us as His creation. It is a sobering thought: Is God so satisfied with His image in me that He would be willing to sign His creation?

Italian-born Hector Bojardi grew up in a culture of great cooking and took to culinary arts at a young age. After immigrating to the United States when he was 19, he worked in New York restaurants and eventually opened his own restaurant, Il Giardino d'Italia, in Cleveland. His dishes were so popular that regular customers began requesting portions to take home. He boxed up uncooked pasta and cheese and poured his signature sauce into milk bottles. Perhaps you have eaten Hector's food yourself. So pleased was he with his own creation that he proudly placed his own name on the label, spelled phonetically for Americans, of course—Chef Boy-ar-dee.

As kings sealed official decrees, they pressed their royal ring into a warm pool of melted wax. The imprinted insignia signified personal endorsement, authenticity, authority, and ownership. Today the Holy Spirit woos us to receive the imprint of Christ on our lives, our values, our goals, our desires, our leadership style for all to see His authenticity, authority, and owner-ship over us. Are we worthy to receive the imprint?

This is the sentiment of Thomas O. Chisholm's 1897 classic hymn:

Oh! to be like Thee, oh! to be like Thee,
Blessed Redeemer, pure as Thou art;
Come in Thy sweetness, come in Thy fullness;
Stamp Thine own image deep on my heart.[2]

The authenticity of His stamp on the lives of holy leaders will be seen in how we love God and our neighbors as ourselves. The litmus test is simply stated: Am I like Christ?

When we as leaders connect to the power source of the Holy Spirit for direction, He empowers us to live out the in-tended purposes of our lives individually and corporately. Our abilities, knowledge, wisdom, and decisions are informed for our personal mission as a child of God and as a leader within the forum where God has strategically placed us for His purposes.

Insecurity about self-preservation has led some of the most unlikely leaders to seek direction from those least qualified to give advice. Nancy Reagan regularly sought counsel from a San Francisco astrologer, after she believed that the attempted assas-sination on President Reagan could have been averted had she consulted astrology. We shudder to know now that she passed instructions from this adviser to the leader of the Free World, determining much of his presidential public appearances.

Even King Saul, terrorized by the Philistine army, resorted to consultation with the witch of Endor, who summoned Samuel from the dead to direct Saul.

> Samuel said, "Why do you consult me, now that the LORD has turned away from you and become your enemy?

The LORD has done what he predicted through me. The
LORD has torn the kingdom out of your hands and given it
to one of your neighbors—to David" *(1 Samuel 28:16-17).*

God despises horoscopes, fortune-tellers, and the occult
precisely because they usurp the rightful position of the Holy
Spirit, who is the only One authorized to tell us what is to come.
"He will speak only what he hears, and he will tell you what is
yet to come" (John 16:13).

In the same way, human advisors, stock projections, educational consultants, and church growth seminars can never
replace the empowerment of the Holy Spirit. When they advise
in conjunction with the voice of the Spirit, when their counsel
lines up with what the Spirit is telling us, they may confirm but
never replace the authority of the Holy Spirit. When we ask for
His counsel, He will tell us of things to come only as it benefits
His mission lived out in our leadership.

Through the Spirit, we are empowered to move from planning to action, from prayer to progress. The disciples were
instructed to wait on the Holy Spirit, to be in prayer and one accord. But when the Holy Spirit was poured out upon them, they
were propelled into action. No longer could they stay in their
own spiritual huddles. In the power of His Spirit, they infiltrated
their society as the Body of Christ.

Into the streets, surrounded by the very people who had
killed their Christ, the disciples went with boldness. Filled
with the Spirit, Peter was singled out among his peers for holy
leadership. "Then Peter stood up with the Eleven, raised his
voice and addressed the crowd: 'Fellow Jews and all of you who
live in Jerusalem, let me explain this to you; listen carefully to

what I say'" (Acts 2:14). Those who had cried, "Crucify him!" only weeks earlier now asked, "What is going on here? What is happening? And what are we to do?" In the power of the Spirit, Peter preached a message of repentance and baptism and the gift of the Holy Spirit (Acts 2:37-38). In empowered multiplication, the group of 120 became about 3,000 in one day.

Who would not like to see corporate profits, student test scores, family checkbooks, or church attendance rise with that kind of dramatic results? We are not guaranteed a power for success. The Holy Spirit is not a red tie or a dress-for-success gimmick. We are, however, guaranteed supernatural power to become His witnesses in whatever leadership venue He has placed us—power to accomplish His mission over our enterprises.

The disciples were called to go into Jerusalem first—the very city where they had failed, denied, betrayed, and scattered. They were to go back into those streets to those same people to display the power of the Holy Spirit as changed persons, to be a flesh-and-blood witness of the transformation only He can make in our lives.

They were to go to Judea, where people were unbelieving, resistant, and skeptical. They were to go to Samaria to serve the disenfranchised, imprisoned, homeless, and those without justice. They were to show mercy and grace in the power of the Holy Spirit. And they were to go to the ends of the earth, as far as they could travel or send the message. This was not a multiple choice, pick-your-favorite-answer option. This was an imperative command, the direct result of the empowerment of the Holy Spirit upon the leaders Jesus left to carry out His mission.

You will receive power when the Holy Spirit comes on you; and you *will be* my witnesses in Jerusalem, and in all

Judea and Samaria, and to the ends of the earth *(Acts 1:8, emphasis added)*.

In one of the most scathing indictments on the Church ever spoken, A. W. Tozer said that if God withdrew His Spirit, 95 percent of what churches do would continue to be done. Are we operating on our own strength, informed by human advisors, going through the motions as man-appointed leaders? Or are we filled with His Spirit empowered for His mission?

The Spruce Goose never served its purpose. It never carried troops or tanks or supplies. It never flew to the war's front or participated in strategic maneuvers. It never fulfilled its creator's dream of helping end the war. Today it maintains its stationary position in a warehouse in McMinnville, Oregon, relegated to entertaining tourists who come to gawk at its enormous investment, monstrous size, and wasted workmanship that accomplished nothing. It was woefully underpowered.

Imagine your office, your classroom, your family dining room, your boardroom, your church sanctuary. Imagine walking into that room engulfed in darkness so thick that you cannot see to take a single step forward. Imagine with the simple flip of a switch flooding the room with light—light that comes through conduit connected to a powerful electric transformer, light that illuminates the open path where you can safely take the next step. Our God is "able to do immeasurably more than all we ask or imagine, according to his power that is at work within us." Why? To bring Him "glory in the church and in Christ Jesus throughout all generations, for ever and ever! Amen" (Ephesians 3:20-21).

The Great Transformer is eagerly waiting to provide power beyond your imagination for holy leadership. Connect to the Source.

CHAPTER FOUR

GO TOGETHER

Berlin is an eclectic city of historical and modern, with ancient Baroque and Italian Renaissance architecture standing next to contemporary sleek steel structures. A statue to Frederick the Great that was begun in 1839 and took nearly 70 years, 40 artists, and 100 designs, pays homage to Germany's grandeur, while nearby 20th-century remnants of the Berlin Wall serve as commitments to learn from a more sordid past. The sky over the Alexanderplatz is punctuated by both the modern TV tower, one of the tallest structures in all of Europe, and the spire of a Lutheran church built in 1270. Where war bombs struck destruction, new construction stands alongside century-old spared architecture.

The Kurfürstendamm, or simply Ku'damm, as it is widely known, is Berlin's most popular shopping street. Stretching for two miles and fashioned after Paris's famed Champs-Élysées, the Ku'damm boulevard is flanked by shops, hotels, and restaurants, considered the center of West Germany during the Cold War and still one of the most fashionable and prestigious areas of the entire city of Berlin. Here is found the most striking, silence-inspiring juxtapositions of old and new: the Kaiser-Wilhelm-Gedächtniskirche or Kaiser Wilhelm Memorial Church, one of Berlin's most famous landmarks.

The neo-Romanesque church was built between 1891 and 1895 as a symbol of Prussian unity by Kaiser Wilhelm II, in honor of his grandfather Kaiser Wilhelm I. A massive structure, the main spire stretched 370 feet above the nave, which seated over 2,000 people. Today it is a tiny specter of its former glory, the result of a 1943 air raid that left only the bottom of the west tower spire, snapped off like a hollow tooth and the small entrance hall just below it. A perfectly round gaping hole exists just below the spire where a masterpiece of stained glass formerly stood above its main entry doors. The remains were scheduled to be demolished, just as the rest of Berlin's casualties had been, in favor of forgetting the old and moving on with new construction. But a campaign arose to preserve the badly damaged remains and instead to build around them. The crippled church is now flanked by steel and concrete honeycombed structures filled with blue glass: an octagonal church to the west and a hexagonal bell tower and small rectangular chapel to the east built on the site of the former nave. The anomaly of the bombed ruins and contemporary modern architecture, now commonly known as the Memorial Church, is an icon of peace and reconciliation, a return to the original intent of the church's symbol—unity.

The church is neither steel and glass nor marble and granite. The Church is the Body of Christ, the community of believers who confess Jesus as Lord. Like the buildings where this community gathers to worship, we can be symbols of destruction and war or living memorials to peace and reconciliation. Like any other enterprise, the message our segment of the Body of Christ communicates to the wider community rises and falls on leadership.

Living together as a family requires from husband, wife, and children a commitment to unity, mutual love, listening, a careful balance of giving and taking, and leadership. So it is as we live together in the family of God. Leaders are charged to guide the body in exercising constant commitment to the building up of one another, submission of our wills to the greater good, and service to one another in mutual bonds of leadership under the directorship of Christ, who established the Church.

Christ loved the church and gave himself up for her to make her holy, cleansing her by the washing with water through the word, and to present her to himself as a radiant church, without stain or wrinkle or any other blemish, but holy and blameless *(Ephesians 5:25-27).*

Just as Christ established the Church, so He provided from the beginning for its leadership. "I tell you that you are Peter, and on this rock I will build my church, and the gates of Hades will not overcome it" (Matthew 16:18).

The divine plan for leadership within His kingdom on earth included from the beginning God-called ministers and laypeople, both given specific roles. He called apostles to direct the Church, to give it guidance, to counsel it, and to admonish and correct it.

It was he who gave some to be apostles, some to be prophets, some to be evangelists, and some to be pastors and teachers *(Ephesians 4:11).*

The assignment given to the apostles, prophets, evangelists, pastors, and teachers clearly identifies the cohesive teamwork planned between clergy and laity:

> Prepare God's people for works of service, so that the body of Christ may be built up until we all reach unity in the faith and in the knowledge of the Son of God and become mature, attaining to the whole measure of the fullness of Christ *(Ephesians 4:12-13)*.

God called lay leaders to come alongside ministers to provide aid, to serve in designated roles, and to carry out the functions that otherwise prohibited the ministers from fulfilling their God-appointed tasks. The story in Acts from the Early Church is a model for the Kingdom throughout time. Where conflict occurs, godly leaders seek a solution that is consistent with God's leadership paradigm for the Church:

> During this time, as the disciples were increasing in numbers by leaps and bounds, hard feelings developed among the Greek-speaking believers—"Hellenists"—toward the Hebrew-speaking believers because their widows were being discriminated against in the daily food lines. So the Twelve called a meeting of the disciples. They said, "It wouldn't be right for us to abandon our responsibilities for preaching and teaching the Word of God to help with the care of the poor" *(Acts 6:1-2, TM)*.

The solution must involve not just any laypeople but lay leaders who display gifts and graces given by the Holy Spirit and a lifestyle exemplary of the current and constant indwelling of the Spirit so that everyone can fulfill his or her God-called assignment:

"So, friends, choose seven men from among you whom everyone trusts, men full of the Holy Spirit and good sense, and we'll assign them this task. Meanwhile, we'll stick to our assigned tasks of prayer and speaking God's Word." The congregation thought this was a great idea. They went ahead and chose—Stephen, a man full of faith and the Holy Spirit, Philip, Procorus, Nicanor, Timon, Parmenas, Nicolas, a convert from Antioch. Then they presented them to the apostles *(vs. 3-6, TM)*.

Leadership designations within the Church, both clergy and lay, must be God-ordained and saturated in prayer: "Praying, the apostles laid on hands and commissioned them for their task" (v. 6, TM).

Biblically accomplished, leadership struggles within the Kingdom are not only resolved; they result in decisions upon which God smiles His approval. The gospel flourishes, new converts are won, and new leaders are called into the ministry.

It takes the entire Body of Christ, living together in unity, to fulfill God's plan for the Church. We are one, but we are many. We are single-minded in our mission, but we are corporate in fulfilling our mission. We sing a unified theme, but we blend our voices in perfect harmony—the soprano and the bass, the alto and the tenor, each with our own gifts of song—to present God's message to the world.

E. Stanley Jones, a 20th century Methodist missionary and theologian, impacts us with a pungent message: "We enter the Kingdom personally, but we live in it corporately." Salvation is individual. Christ calls each of us to personal confession, repentance, and forgiveness of sins. We cannot inherit salvation from our parents; it is not in our DNA and cannot be genetically engineered into our chromosomes. Neither can we be saved by osmosis; salvation cannot come from close association with other believers. We must each make a personal decision to turn from our sins and receive Christ as Lord.

But from there, we leave the individualistic Christian life and enter into the family of God, a lifelong journey with our fellow brothers and sisters within the Body of Christ, where we live together corporately.

According to *Merriam-Webster Online Dictionary*, the word *corporate* derives from the Latin *corporatus*, past participle of *corporare*, which means "to make into a body." All sorts of words suggesting the meaning of *body* come from these shared roots. A *corporation* was first a group of merchants or traders united into a trade guild, and today a corporation is a body formed by law to act as a single person. From *incarnate* to *corpse*, from birth to death, the body—many members forming one whole—is emphasized in the long history of *corporate*. The *incarnation* of Christ is itself a metaphor for how the Church is to live—within the body. We are a body formed to act as a single person.

Today's individualistic emphasis influences us to think of our relationship with Christ as exclusively personal—an ethos of "Jesus and me" in a journey for two. This philosophy tempts us to see the narrow road as a private lane, making our own decisions in a vacuum and looking first to our personal interests. As C. S. Lewis wrote in his book, *The Weight of Glory*, "No Christian and, indeed, no historian could accept the epigram which defines religion as 'what a man does with his solitude.'"

We express our personal faith, but we live out our faith corporately. Leonard Sweet writes in *11 Indispensable Relationships You Can't Be Without*: "The real meaning of life is not a journey question or an arrival question. It's a relationship question. Your journey and your destination are both important, but neither is possible without an answer to this prior question: Who are you taking with you on the journey toward your destination?" The Bible is clear: our journey is both personal and corporate.

Scripture uses several terms to show us the corporate character of the Christian life: We are the Church. We are the community of believers. We are the Body of Christ.

> The body is a unit, though it is made up of many parts; and though all its parts are many, they form one body. So it is with Christ. . . . Now you are the body of Christ, and each one of you is a part of it *(1 Corinthians 12: 12, 27)*.

Of this body, Christ himself is the Head.

> He is the head of the body, the church; he is the beginning and the firstborn from among the dead, so that in everything he might have the supremacy . . . Now I rejoice in what was suffered for you, and I fill up in my flesh what is still lacking in regard to Christ's afflictions, for the sake of his body, which is the church *(Colossians 1: 18, 24)*.

Within the Body and with Him as our Head, our faith adventure with Christ has a corporate character. It is no longer about just "Jesus and me." It is no longer about my desires and interests first, my worship preferences, my opinions, or my ability to control what happens in my local branch of this eternal Body of Christ. Leadership within the Church, both clergy and lay, must be submitted to the direction of the Holy Spirit.

Inherent in the corporate faith is the reality of togetherness. The word *saint* in its singular format appears only three times in the Bible. By contrast, the word in its plural form, *saints*, appears at least 95 times. Where *saints* is written in the New Testament, it refers to the Church—the collective family of God. When we join this community by grace through faith, we are adopted not as an *only* child but as part of a growing, loving family with many brothers and sisters. We are children of God, heirs of God, and joint heirs with Christ.

> You received the Spirit of sonship. And by him we cry, "Abba, Father." The Spirit himself testifies with our spirit that we are God's children. Now if we are children, then we are heirs—heirs of God and co-heirs with Christ *(Romans 8:15-17)*.

The New Testament Church was formed by a God-design: "All the believers were together and had everything in common" (Acts 2:44). In far too many churches today, where wars rage and battle lines are drawn as people jockey for leadership control, this New Testament picture is foreign. People who feel powerless at home or at work find in the church their own little kingdoms over which they can hold complete sway. Many churches are small for a reason, as leaders fear the threats of new people to their bastions of control. We (the Leonards) recall the couple who sat in our living room and, oblivious to their own self-centered confession, stated, "What has happened to our church? We used to control everything here, but not any more." Sadly, in too many cases, we have difficulty singing with gusto: "'Tis a glorious Church, without spot or wrinkle."[1]

Being together and holding everything in common means erasing territory boundaries, tearing down self-made divisions of labor. In every arm of the Kingdom—in the local church, in international ministry offices, in mission regions, in Christian universities and theological seminaries—it means less competition and more collaboration, less control and more corporateness. It means living out on a daily basis for the whole world to see the togetherness of Christ's Body.

Holding all things in common includes authority. It takes all of us, clergy and lay, working together in tandem, creating synergy in an orchestrated dance of authority and submission to see His kingdom come to earth. Together, keenly aware of the eternal consequences of God-entrusted leadership within His Body, we must hold lightly the *power* of leadership and hold closely the awesome *responsibility* entrusted to us to lead.

In determining the careful balancing of authority and responsibility as leaders within the Kingdom, we cannot claim immunity from the cataclysmic change in attitudes about authority that shook our society in the 1960s, a shift from which there appears to be no return.

Unfortunately, too many of our churches today in the third millennia of Christianity seem at best remotely related to the New Testament Church. As the society changes, the Church reflects those changes because we are a body of human beings influenced in our thinking by our contemporary culture. Pre-1960s, we lived in a world of accepted authoritarianism in government, in business, in schools, and even often in homes. When authoritarianism worked in the society, it worked, however well or poorly, in the Church. But no longer.

According to David Quinn, Irish columnist and commentator on religious and social affairs, in "Authority—Yes, Authoritarianism—No," the challenge to authoritarianism that began in the 18th-century Enlightenment did not fully come of age until the explosion of the 1960s, when rebellion against authority in every venue turned society upside down.

If the pre-modern era was punctuated by a submissive attitude to authority, whether it be that of parents, teachers, priests, etc., then the modern is punctuated by rebellion against authority. If in the pre-modern era we were taught not to question, in the modern era we question all the presuppositions of our forebears, although not, alas, our own presuppositions. If in the pre-modern world authority all too often slipped over into authoritarianism and the rule of fear, in the modern era all forms of authority, with the possible exception of the natural sciences, have been undermined.

Quinn goes on to say that the demise of an authoritarian society is not necessarily to be mourned. Even Dietrich Bonhoeffer, 20th century German theologian and martyr, claimed: "Man has come of age." However, with the widespread rebellion of authority came an indiscriminate *no* to all authority and *yes* to absolute freedom. Society taught that we could question the authority even of absolute truth and morality. This affected both the Church's leadership roles and its role of authority in proclaiming inherent values and beliefs.

If the Church has learned anything from the post-1960s rebellion of authoritarianism, it should be that we must earn the right to lead. Autocratic leaders are a mockery to God and a failure to laity and ministers who have God-given gifts to think without being told what to think. Roles and titles within the

Kingdom, denominations, and local churches do not come with the automatic authoritarian right to speak for God. Very few of us have the true gift of prophecy, and biblical history records that those who did were generally stoned, not elected or appointed to higher positions of authority. Indeed, within the body of Christ, autocratic leadership is an oxymoron.

The page on the calendar has turned when church leaders could make solitary decisions, act on impulse, and dictate how other persons should fulfill the will of God in ministry or lay leadership roles. Today the only person an autocratic leader will lead is himself or herself.

Spirit-filled pastors as leaders and shepherds of local congregations are chosen by God and confirmed by the people. They are entrusted with the responsibility to cast and tender the vision for the Body. When people are cantankerous, when finances are challenging, when facilities are inadequate, the mission is still the same. Pastors must proceed with a sense of God-calling, God-enabling leadership.

Without the daily infilling of the Holy Spirit, they become dictatorial, governing with "divide and conquer" mentality. But as they seek the Holy Spirit, they are guided to lead with authority, not with authoritarianism or with a heavy-handed, Scripture-plucking defense. In true holiness, they lead their congregations in "paths of righteousness," emulating the Good Shepherd, who leads not for personal ego or with condescension but rather out of love for the benefit and safety of His flock:

> GOD, my shepherd! I don't need a thing. You have bedded me down in lush meadows, you find me quiet pools to drink from. True to your word, you let me catch my breath and send me in the right direction. Even when the way goes through

Death Valley, I'm not afraid when you walk at my side. Your trusty shepherd's crook makes me feel secure. You serve me a six-course dinner right in front of my enemies. You revive my drooping head; my cup brims with blessing. Your beauty and love chase after me every day of my life. I'm back home in the house of GOD for the rest of my life *(Psalm 23, TM)*.

The laity is equally God-called to become workers in His vineyard in tandem with the pastor and the cast vision: "For we are labourers together with God" (1 Corinthians 3:9, KJV). Where laypeople fail to serve as willing volunteers, they become spiritually lazy, a key target for Satan, who waits ever-ready to prompt them with tools of criticism and judgmentalism. They turn inward, becoming consumeristic. They are obsessed with self-health; like those who constantly monitor their own temperature and blood-pressure, they ask, "Are my needs being met? Am I being fed? Do I feel good about what is going on here?" Before they know it, they are back on the "Jesus and me" private path instead of interwoven in the corporate Body of Christ and consumed with *esprit de corps* for His Kingdom. Only when filled with the Spirit are they enabled to serve as holy leaders with holy intent, even as our Master did.

How is this possible? The Holy Spirit can daily transform our individual-oriented inwardness to a corporate oneness in Christ. This unity produces a community of shared life and purpose so that our desires are melded together as one. When Paul wrote to the Corinthians that "God has combined the members of the body" (1 Corinthians 12:24), the word we read as *combined* was translated from the Greek meaning *blended*. Like separate ingredients poured together in a blender, we are combined in such a way that our distinct flavors and textures may stand out, but no single ingredient is any longer visible.

According to Ray Kurzweil, today's technological and societal changes catapult us forward at ever-increasing speed into the future, "so rapid and profound it represents a rupture in the fabric of human history." Change is occurring at an exponential rather than a linear rate. In simple terms, the rate of progress is not constant. The development of sharp-edged tools and the wheel took thousands of years, while the Industrial Age completely revolutionized our world in only a century, affecting almost every area of daily life in some way. Innovations of the first 20 years of the 20th century eclipsed all the advances of the 19th century combined. Today the volume of information is doubling every two years, and changes that previously spanned a full a generation to take effect now happen every five years. Our world spins ever faster in the development of "necessities" that did not even exist a year ago.

To borrow an analogy from Harold Graves Jr., president of Nazarene Bible College, if you lived in 1967 and wanted to listen to Elvis Presley sing "He Touched Me," you would have placed an LP on your record player. In the 1970s to listen to the same song, you could have bought a new 8-track tape for your player. In the 1980s you might have moved up to the cassette tape player, and in the 1990s you would have listened to Elvis sing "He Touched Me" on a compact disc player. Today almost all of these are relics of antique stores or flea markets. A CD and a CD player, even the portable Walkman, are far too cumbersome, and where would you find time in your hectic lifestyle to go to the store to make your purchase anyway? So you download "He Touched Me" in enhanced sound from iTunes to your iPod. Who knows how you will access Elvis next year?

The question is not whether the world is speeding away from us in technology. The question is not even how fast the pace of progress is. The question is whether we will adapt to the exponential rate of progress. How does this affect leadership within the Kingdom?

The quality of attention to leadership is directly proportionate to the amount of discretionary time a person has to give to the organization. In today's over-calendared, under-rested lifestyle, each of us, whether CEO or stay-at-home parent, has become more tightly restricted in delegation of our time. These societal shifts mirrored in the leadership of the church appear in a growing phenomenon: the board-led church is giving way to the staff-led church.

In a simpler, slower-paced time, lay leaders were able not only to tithe their time but also to invest heavily both in performing duties and in developing strategy. As daily demands of life grow, the reality of our fast-paced society has greatly impacted the direct, hand-on leadership roles of lay persons and delegated more of the direction-setting to the clergy. For example, previously choir members could not only attend rehearsals but could also participate in the development of the music program, just as finance committee members only a few years ago could not only hear reports and give input but could hands-on develop the church's annual budget. This phenomenon is fed by increasing numbers of churches of all sizes adding pastoral staff and the growth of larger churches with vast arrays of ministries.

Today as churches bridge this societal leap imposed by slamming schedules, increased numbers of choices, and technological specialization, Satan stands close by to stir the pot. The "Jesus and me" ethos, even within the context of a body of believers, searches first for what I want, what my role is, and where my power is being threatened. The corporate "Jesus and us" mentality looks for how I can best serve, what I can contribute, and where my gifts can augment those who have been called to full-time service.

In all cases, there must be mutual submission and respect among clergy and laity as well as within the body of lay leaders. Pastors and pastoral staff must provide leadership, vision, organization, and inspiration to the ministry teams of laity. Those who take on more responsibility are called to higher accountability, and those who serve as partners in ministry must hold leaders to a high standard of ethics and motives. In all things, the Body of Christ must function with all members completing to the best of their abilities the ministry leadership roles to which they are called:

> Now you are the body of Christ, and each one of you is a part of it. And in the church God has appointed first of all apostles, second prophets, third teachers, then workers of miracles, also those having gifts of healing, those able to help others, those with gifts of administration, and those speaking in different kinds of tongues *(1 Corinthians 12:27-28).*

As Thomas Friedman wrote in *The World Is Flat 3.0,* "The best companies are the best collaborators. In the flat world, more and more business will be done through collaborations within and between companies." The Kingdom is at its best when we collaborate, each leader bringing his or her gifts and skills at the involvement level of his or her ability. We operate as a team, not as opposing single players. We combine advice, knowledge, expertise, and experience to become the best the Church can be.

How can we best join our efforts as leaders within the Kingdom to become a more perfect Bride of Christ?

We must worship together. Genuine collective worship levels all playing fields of leadership. We are all equal as we turn our eyes and hearts to God. We cannot be consumed with our selfish needs, our petty issues, or our competition with our next-pew-neighbor if we are truly focused on God. He inhabits the praise of His people. The joy of our transformation by grace in salvation finds its expression in true worship.

> A time is coming and has now come when the true worshipers will worship the Father in spirit and truth, for they are the kind of worshipers the Father seeks. God is spirit, and his worshipers must worship in spirit and in truth *(John 4:23-24)*.

Corporately we honor God's grace, mercy, and love. Together we celebrate His hope as we lift and encourage one another in the disparaging moments of life. Together we recognize the presence and glory of God among us. Together we offer our confessions and our adoration. Together we express our beliefs. There is collective power in reciting the Apostles' Creed in unison. Through our expressions of praise, honor, confession, and confirmation of belief in who He is, God is glorified, and even those who do not know Him recognize when He is present. Fueled by the Holy Spirit, holy leaders lead in worshiping, whether on the platform or in the pew, regardless the setting or personal preferences.

We must give together. Stewardship is about Lordship. God owns all, and we simply ask the Owner what He would like us to do with all His resources. We cannot give generously as He wants without worshiping. We cannot worship without giving generously as He wants.

Together we support one another and the Kingdom. We supply the needs of the marginalized and disenfranchised. We support the mission of taking the gospel to the whole world. We give personally, but we support God's Kingdom collectively, not individually. Our gifts combined with those of our brothers and sisters are multiplied exponentially like loaves and fish. We are not independent; we are interdependent. Fueled by the Holy Spirit, holy leaders lead in giving freely, sacrificially, and with a joyful spirit.

We must live in unity together. The New Testament Church was together daily. They were in one accord, united in spirit. They shared all things of life in common, caring for one another's needs, living at peace because of the Holy Spirit's power that had cleansed them of selfish, individual interests. God cannot bless a church that is divided in its leadership. We must resolve differences through the power of the Holy Spirit and focus on unity over personal preferences, not as individuals but as a corporate body blended together in peace, each one seeking to serve the needs of the other.

The Kingdom is a blending of unique individuals, a mystery of Christ's power to make us one. In the tune of W. Somerset Maugham, who is attributed to saying, "The essence of the beautiful is unity in variety," we are enriched by diversity and bonded in unity. What holds us together in the Church is stronger than what distinguishes us. Fueled by the Holy Spirit, holy leaders foster a culture of unity, serving and submitting to one another.

We must pray together. We pray for one another's needs, but we pray most that we will become more like Christ, model His lifestyle, take on His values, and adopt His mission. William McGill, former president of Columbia University, said, "The value of consistent prayer is not that He will hear us, but that we will hear Him." Every revival and every movement of God was predicated by prayer. Fueled by the Holy Spirit, holy leaders consistently spend concerted time in personal and intercessory prayer and serve one another as steadfast prayer partners.

We must make disciples together. Our mission today is the same that Christ gave to all His followers: "Go and make disciples of all nations, baptizing them in the name of the Father and of the Son and of the Holy Spirit, and teaching them to obey everything I have commanded you" (Matthew 28:19-20).

C. S. Lewis in his book *The Weight of Glory* discussed Christians' desires. He said they are not too strong but rather too weak: "We are far too easily pleased." We must do more than assemble together to call ourselves the kingdom of God. We must be reaching people who do not know God. We must be disturbed if our churches are barren of sinners seeking transformation. Fueled by the Holy Spirit, holy leaders ask God for a holy dissatisfaction, a yearning that cannot be satisfied until people are brought to Him.

God has given us all the resources we need in order to make disciples for Him. Even within the least equipped, most economically strained church, our gadgets, facilities, staff, technology, and finances far exceed those of the New Testament

Church. Yet those believers held all things in common. Is our church modeling the Great Commission in every ministry and expenditure? Are we reaching externally and focusing outward, or are we turning internal, even as God is bringing the lost right to our doorsteps?

Augustine said, "I had not known Christ, except that the Church had taught me." We thank God for the Church. It taught us personally to know God's transforming power, and we will be forever grateful for the clear proclamation of the gospel and guidance we received there as we entered into salvation.

We owe a debt of gratitude for our heritage, the understanding of what it means today to be a part of His kingdom, and our commitment to the vision of tomorrow. We must live with a continuous, intentional awareness of our mission to make Christlike disciples in the nations. We must be constantly reminded that it is not about me; it is about the corporate Body of Christ.

The Berlin Memorial Church on the tree-lined Ku'damm boulevard is not a museum. It is not a monument to war or to peace. It is the structural embodiment of Christ's words: "I will build my church, and the gates of Hades will not overcome it" (Matthew 16:18). Broken and hollow neo-Renaissance ruins alongside contemporary steel and glass architecture form the reminder that as the various parts of the Body of Christ, we are blended together. We are many, yet we are one. We are broken, yet we triumph.

In a divine mystery, when we put our strengths and abilities together with God, the mission is accomplished, the gospel is proclaimed, and the Kingdom is extended. Together we withstand all.

According to an African proverb, "If you want to travel fast, go alone. If you want to travel far, go together."

This is not a solo path but a togetherness journey! Do not be fooled by our narcissistic culture. It is not about "Jesus and me." Our faith expressed in holy love and obedience in the ultimate journey of leadership under the Lordship of Christ is about "Jesus and us." Go together.

CHAPTER FIVE

CHOOSE FOR YOUR HOUSE

In the foothills of the Ozark Mountains, just inside the
Arkansas border across from the glassy waters of Table Rock
Lake, surrounded by pines pointing to the lazy clouds, lies the
picturesque town of Eureka Springs. It's really somewhat of a
fairy tale town, one built for real people of another era but preserved for modern-day tourists. Victorian houses, transformed
into gift shops, boutiques, and bed-and-breakfast inns, abound
in pink, turquoise, green, and blue with turrets and towers,
sweeping front porches with white railings, and an abundance of
gingerbread trim. The streets wind snakelike up the side of the
hill, beaconing the visitor on to just one more street for more of
the same—tea rooms with lace and lavender, antique glassware
and vintage photo postcards, and candy—fudge, salt water taffy,
fudge, homemade caramels, and more fudge.

The people who settled here and built these winding roads
and Victorian houses came because of the springs. Natural hot
water springs full of healthy minerals bubbled to the surface,
and many came to bathe in them and to drink from them for

their medicinal value. Some found a measure of healing and stayed. They built homes, businesses, and eventually a town that grew into a city. The preserved quaintness of the city grew into an entertainment center and eventually a resort.

We have visited Eureka Springs, enjoying the tea rooms and shops. But each time we would ask a store or hotel clerk, "Where are the springs?" each would reply in embarrassment, "I'm sorry, but I don't know. I really can't tell you." Throughout the years, though the historic homes and hotels were transferred from one generation to another, the foundational information, the real reason for the existence of Eureka Springs, Arkansas, was not.

The Israelites were steeped in their history. They knew who they were and from where they had come. They passed from one generation to another the essential story of their existence and in so doing transferred their identity and character. This was all God's planning.

When the Israelites came to the Jordan to cross over into the Promised Land, they were in uncharted territory. Joshua gave them divinely inspired direction:

> When you see the ark of the covenant of the LORD your God, and the priests, who are Levites, carrying it, you are to move out from your positions and follow it. Then you will know which way to go, since you have never been this way before (*Joshua 3:3-4*).

Though the Jordan River was at flood stage, when the priests carrying the ark of the covenant touched their feet to the water's edge, the water from upstream piled up in a heap, and all the people crossed over opposite Jericho. The priests stood on dry ground in the middle of the Jordan until the entire nation of people had passed by. Then before their eyes the waters returned and ran at full flood stage as before.

But before they left the dry river bed, God instructed Joshua to call together one man from each of the 12 tribes to walk back into the river's path and pick up one stone each that otherwise would have lain to this day at the bottom of the Jordan. They placed these 12 stone on the other side of the river bank. We do not know today exactly how these stones were arranged, but we do know why:

> Each of you is to take up a stone on his shoulder, according to the number of the tribes of the Israelites, to serve as a sign among you. In the future, when your children ask you, "What do these stones mean?" tell them that the flow of the Jordan was cut off before the ark of the covenant of the LORD. When it crossed the Jordan, the waters of the Jordan were cut off. These stones are to be a memorial to the people of Israel forever (*Joshua 4:5-7*).

God is big on story, and He wants His story communicated. His story is of His Creation and His covenant with Abraham and his descendants. His story is of His Son and a better and lasting covenant. He wants His people to know, to remember, and to pass on His story.

> Love the LORD your God with all your heart and with all your soul and with all your strength. These commandments that I give you today are to be upon your hearts. Impress them on your children. Talk about them when you sit at home and when you walk along the road, when you lie down and when you get up. Tie them as symbols on your hands and

bind them on your foreheads. Write them on the doorframes
of your houses and on your gates *(Deuteronomy 6:5-9)*.

In the future, when your son asks you, "What is the
meaning of the stipulations, decrees and laws the LORD our
God has commanded you?" tell him: "We were slaves of
Pharaoh in Egypt, but the LORD brought us out of Egypt
with a mighty hand. Before our eyes the LORD sent miraculous signs and wonders—great and terrible—upon Egypt
and Pharaoh and his whole household. But he brought us
out from there to bring us in and give us the land that he
promised on oath to our forefathers" *(Deut. 6:20-23)*.

The people who were privileged to witness this miracle saw,
knew, and would never forget. But they were charged with the
responsibility of teaching those who would come after them,
who would know only because leaders taught, guided, and reminded them of God's intervention. God commissioned leaders
within the family.

Far too often we fall into erroneous thinking that home
is where we live with our family, and work is where we go to
fulfill our leadership responsibilities. But the family is in fact our
greatest leadership arena and where our most important leadership responsibilities lie. We've heard it said that our most basic
instinct is not for survival but for family. Most of us would give
our lives for a family member, yet we often take our family for
granted. If you rate your leadership skills at church or at work
highly, if a team or a classroom of students looks to you for leadership, are you putting equal emphasis on your God-appointed
role as a leader in the family? Are you satisfied with your leadership performance at home?

To understand, we go back to the Creation story, to the beginning of the beginning, to the first words of God's written Word. We can learn much about God's plan for leadership within the family by carefully analyzing this story. As two former English teachers and students of literature, we (the authors) recognize that Genesis 1 is a poem. There is a stylistic pattern to the arrangement of the verses and a repetitive cadence to its words. The repetition of style emphasizes the portions of the Creation story that are to be understood as parallel events, pieces of which we are to take particular note, patterns that tell us about the nature of the Creator God and of His plan for humanity:

And God said, "Let there be light," and there was light *(v. 3)*.

And God said, "Let there be an expanse between the waters" . . . And it was so *(vv. 6-7)*.

And God said, "Let the water under the sky be gathered to one place, and let dry ground appear." And it was so *(v. 9)*.

And so on.

The cadence continues in His naming. God is interested in words. He spoke the world into being, and He spoke names for each part of His creation in a parallel cadence:

God called the light "day," and the darkness he called "night" *(v. 5)*.

God called the expanse "sky" *(v. 8)*.

God called the dry ground "land," and the gathered waters he called "seas" *(v. 10)*.

And so on.

There is also a rhythm in His timing:

And there was evening, and there was morning—the first day *(v. 5)*.

And there was evening, and there was morning—the second day *(v. 8)*.

And there was evening, and there was morning—the third day *(v. 13)*.

And so on.

God is interested in timing. He created an orderly, timely world for His people. He inspected His own handiwork and called it "good" *(vv. 4, 10, 12, 18, 21, 25)*.

Even before the creation of Eve and the establishment of the family, Adam was clearly the first leader in recorded history. God brought before him all of the fish, birds, and creatures of the earth for him to examine and name. We sometimes laugh that Adam must have exhibited a little trouble or at least a bit of fatigue with this challenge, because God decided Adam needed a helper. God established the first family for companionship:

It is not good for the man to be alone. I will make a helper suitable for him. . . . The man said, "This is now bone of my bones and flesh of my flesh; she shall be called 'woman,' for she was taken out of man" *(Genesis 2:18, 23)*.

God saw *all* that he had made, and it was very good
(1:31, emphasis added).

This "and so on" God is a God of consistency. Our God is
a God of order and planning, of precision and timing, of com-
pleteness and goodness. His plan for the family produced the
world's first institution. His design for leadership within the
family was orderly, precise, complete, and good.

God blessed them and gave them their purpose:

Be fruitful and increase in number; fill the earth and subdue
it. Rule over the fish of the sea and the birds of the air and over
every living creature that moves on the ground *(Genesis 1:28).*

By instructing them together to subdue the earth and to
rule over all God's creation, He was clearly giving them leadership roles. Before this point in the Creation saga, the animals
belonged to God, just as the man and woman did. Humankind
had no right to interfere or to direct them. Though Adam had
been given the privilege of naming them, he and the rest of
God's creation were on a separate although unequal footing. But
with the spoken Word of God to subdue and rule, and as the
King James Version puts it "have dominion over" them as a king
would over a kingdom, a hierarchy of leadership was established.
Made in His likeness, man and woman would now share in the
image of His authoritative nature. They would be leaders.

The family was God's first arena for this display of His
power in holy leadership. From the Garden forward, God has
instructed us in His Word how the family is to interact with one
another in perfect balance of authority and submission, of dominion and compassion. Now thousands of years later, in spite

of cultural and secular forces, regardless of technological and educational advances, God's plan for the family can no more be changed from His creative purpose by humanistic philosophies or lobbyists than the sun or the moon can be altered by scientists and astronomers. But that has not kept them from trying.

Rebellion against God's plan has brought us a varied tapestry of "the family" that some would proudly call progressive, open-minded, and tolerant. The fallout affects the innocent picking up the pieces of a broken home and spreads across generations through no choice of their own: children with two daddies or two mommies, single moms and single dads raising children alone, children maintaining two complete sets of clothing and personal items, shuttled between two homes on a weekly basis by court order to separated parents with joint child custody.

The staggering statistics of those who have tried to alter God's Creation plan for the family change so rapidly that truly accurate data changes at Internet speed, rather than book publication speed. According to cultural commentator Chuck Colson's *Cohabitation: It's Training for Divorce*, between 1960 and 2004 the number of unmarried couples living together in the United States increased by over 1,200 percent. In 2004 there were 5,080,000 cohabitating unmarried couples in the United States. Statistics show that those who live together before marriage are almost twice as likely to divorce as those who do not live together. Jennifer Baker of the Forest Institute of Professional Psychology in Springfield, Missouri, reports that the divorce rate in America is 50 percent of first marriages, 67 percent of second marriages, and 74 percent of third marriages.[1]

Clearly, the nuclear family as God created it to be is in a meltdown. We are moving toward a post-family society. Some would say we have already arrived.

Though humankind can rebel, alter, and rewrite the parameters for the family, no one can change the intended creation of the institution of the family. Authors have filled volumes, and therapists and counselors have collected millions of dollars trying to provide reasons the family seems to be unraveling before our very eyes. Because God is the divine Author of the family and its divinely oriented leadership roles, and because the Holy Spirit is the divine Counselor, His Word is still the greatest manual for providing authentic, divine guidance for us as leaders. While some have been affected through no fault of their own, all must look for divine help to be the holy leaders within the home God created us to be.

Erma Bombeck, renowned syndicated columnist and humorist, wrote, "The family. We were a strange little band of characters trudging through life sharing diseases and toothpaste, coveting one another's desserts, hiding shampoo, borrowing money, locking each other out of our rooms, inflicting pain and kissing to heal it in the same instant, loving, laughing, defending, and trying to figure out the common thread that bound us all together."

According to *Merriam-Webster Online Dictionary*, the word *family* evolved from Middle English *familie*, first appearing about the 15th century. It derived from the Latin *familia*, meaning "household," which included servants as well as kinsmen of the householder. The farthest back we can trace its roots is *famulus*, which is literally translated "servant." God called His first created institution "family," because we are a household of servants, each serving the other. We are to be authentic servant leaders within the family.

Adam and Eve were like half-circles, each incomplete without the other. Marriage was the culmination of God's full creative plan whereby each would serve the other and the circle would be complete. God's gift of sexuality provided for one flesh, the apex of their relationship expressed in joy. Though polygamy exists in Old Testament stories, not one of those relationships ended in joy. Without exception, they produced strife. Monogamy is the only God-given context for one flesh. It is not cultural or genetic; it is Creation.

The concept of leadership within the family has been misused and abused by a dogmatic and imperialistic wielding of scriptures like Ephesians 5 as both a weapon and a shield. While the Bible is intended primarily for our spiritual understanding and not to teach us manners, culture, or science, God inspired the words of Ephesians to portray not only contemporary manners but also to provide timeless, cross-cultural guidelines for family leadership. As a result, through chapters five and six, husbands, wives, fathers, mothers, grandparents, aunts, uncles, singles, children—*all* the family—can discover God's plan for their leadership roles.

The relationship of husband and wife is fashioned after the relationship of Christ and the Church. Indeed, Ephesians 5 is really church language. We often read it as marriage instructions explained by the metaphor of Christ and the Church when it is really the other way around: this is Church language explained by the metaphor of how family members are to relate to one another.

Out of respect for Christ, be courteously reverent to one another. Wives, understand and support your husbands in ways that show your support for Christ. The husband provides leadership to his wife the way Christ does to his church, not by domineering but by cherishing. So just as the church submits to Christ as he exercises such leadership, wives should likewise submit to their husbands. Husbands, go all out in your love for your wives, exactly as Christ did for the church—a love marked by giving, not getting. Christ's love makes the church whole. His words evoke her beauty. Everything he does and says is designed to bring the best out of her, dressing her in dazzling white silk, radiant with holiness. And that is how husbands ought to love their wives. They're really doing themselves a favor—since they're already "one" in marriage. No one abuses his own body, does he? No, he feeds and pampers it. That's how Christ treats us, the church, since we are part of his body. And this is why a man leaves father and mother and cherishes his wife. No longer two, they become "one flesh." *This is a huge mystery, and I don't pretend to understand it all. What is clearest to me is the way Christ treats the church. And this provides a good picture of how each husband is to treat his wife, loving himself in loving her, and how each wife is to honor her husband* (Ephesians 5:21-33, TM, emphasis added).

If we want to understand God's plan for relationships within the family, we must seek to understand Christ's relationship with the Church. Then we have the perfect model for our homes and the basis of our leadership roles there.

The husband is called to be the band around the house. He must be a steadying influence, a security force that holds the home together. His standards are almost impossibly high, yet God equips him to fulfill the calling. When we envision Christ dying an agonizing death on the Cross, giving His life for the Church He loved, is it possible for a mere human being to love his wife with equal dedication, passion, and selflessness? Certainly not through his own capabilities. In fact, this kind of *agape*, unconditional love, is precisely impossible humanly. The power to do so is available only through the infilling of the Holy Spirit.

Wives are called to honor their husbands. Selfless love expresses itself in ultimate respect. Second only to her reverence for God, her loyalty must be to him above all other relationships. Can she achieve this submission alone? Only the Holy Spirit enables her to do what she otherwise cannot accomplish.

Husbands and wives are to lead by loving. To love your husband or wife sounds simple, yet it is as complex as loving yourself, as deep as Christ's love for the Church—"a profound mystery" (v. 32). Loving means being interested in what interests your spouse, seeking what pleases him or her. Unconditional love, just like the love that Christ had for the Church that led Him to the Cross, must precede leading in the family.

Husbands and wives must be faithful to one another. We are instructed to leave our former relationships of mother and father and to "cleave" (Genesis 2:24, KJV) to one another, to cling to, to be joined to, to be united with, to cherish. As one flesh, we reserve all our affections for the other and are devoted to the other "as to the Lord" (Ephesians 5:22). In the marriage vows we take before God and in the presence of witnesses, we promise to forsake all others, not temporarily but until separated by death. There are no "incompatibility" clauses in God's Word.

Unconditional faithfulness, just as Christ had for the Church, must precede leading in the family.

Husbands and wives must provide for one another. Our provisional responsibilities far eclipse the title of breadwinner. Beyond the material, we must provide mutual emotional support, security, love, loyalty, listening, understanding, faithfulness, reliability, and acceptance. Commitment to provide for one another's needs, just as Christ provided for the Church, must precede leading in the family.

No one owns the other. We are owned by God, and He lends us to each other. The relationship that allows each person to fulfill his or her God-called leadership responsibilities in the home must begin and end with complete submission to God.

In His divine will, God blesses homes with children: "Sons are a heritage from the LORD, children a reward from him" (Psalm 127:3). While we do not understand the heartbreaking mysteries of infertility, miscarriages, and stillborns, we recognize and honor God's sovereignty. A home without children is no less a home, even as single adults comprise a home with God-given leadership roles.

To those entrusted with children come additional responsibilities, even as the children themselves have responsibilities within the home. Children are to obey their parents (Ephesians 6:1) and to honor their father and mother, which is the first of the Ten Commandments that comes with a promise:

> . . . so that you may live long in the land the LORD your God is giving you (Exodus 20:12).

> . . . that it may go well with you and that you may enjoy long life on the earth (Ephesians 6:3).

While these are promises from God, this is a lifestyle that brings its own rewards. Where each member, including children, is fulfilling his or her God-called role within the family, there is peace, harmony, and unity. In every stage of life, at whatever age we are as children of our living parents, we are called to love, respect, and honor them.

Leadership lessons to our children are delivered in the laboratory of life. They are sometimes taught, sometimes caught, sometimes wrought. Our examples in loving, listening, giving, forgiving, respecting, and remaining faithful will last a lifetime.

As in all leadership roles, parents should ask God for wisdom to deal with children. An old proverb says, "In bringing up children, spend on them half as much money and twice as much time." Raising children is a crock pot assignment, not a microwave job. In this hectic, over-calendared society, children need a huge investment of time and influence from holy parent leaders. We must embrace them, take interest in their wholesome activities, attend and cheer on their ball games and band concerts.

We do not profess to have done everything right, but instead of stewing over their friends not all being from the church, we opened our homes to our children's friends. Mignon McLaughlin, American journalist and author, wrote, "If your children spend most of their time in other people's houses, you're lucky; if they all congregate at your house, you're blessed." The Gunter family was known for its cookouts for the baseball team members and a home where all were welcomed. The Leonard household was an open door, a busy swimming pool, and an address the pizza delivery man knew well.

Most leaders lead by one of two styles: control or influence. Every two-year-old wants to control his or her own life. Why do you think they call them the "terrible two's"? Their favorite words are "Mine!" and "No!" We know that when children are young, they must be led by control. Yet which of us has not witnessed the grocery store tantrums in which tiny tyrants rule placating parents, whose only wish is to silence the culprit and exit the store with some measure of dignity left. Too late. Those parents who abdicate the control to children when they are young will likely never be able to retrieve it.

As children mature, they must be led to make choices. When they are toddlers, we dress them for bed, set their bedtime, and tuck them in, regardless of the tears and cajoling for one more drink or one more trip to the bathroom. In time, the bedroom routine can offer them increasing levels of participation in the decision-making process: "Would you like to wear your Bob the Builder pajamas or your Barney pajamas?"

Rose Kennedy, mother of President John F. Kennedy and two other sons who served in the United States Senate, said, "Whenever I held my newborn baby in my arms, I used to think that what I said and did to him could have an influence not only on him but on all whom he met, not only for a day or a month or a year, but for all eternity—a very challenging and exciting thought for a mother." Age by age, little by little, wise parent leadership shifts subtly from control to influence. There comes a stage when we know control will no longer work. In today's society, rebellious teens have a multiplicity of options, even in housing: they don't have to come home. Tom Nees, sociologist and leadership consultant, once said, "Leadership is about people following when they don't have to. That takes influence." He went on to say, "Despite the derailment of puberty, if we have established trust and respect, with God's help and much covering of prayer, they will follow our influence just as they did our control. And when they do not, more prayer will bring more wisdom and more patience as we lovingly wait for the prodigals to come home."

Parent leaders are called by God to exert influence. In nine years as a high school counselor, I (Gunter) worked with students and parents through a multiplicity of challenges. Many of those parents had made conscious decisions not to influence their children but rather to let them make their own choices and thereby learn independence.

The truth is that everything else is already influencing our children: their friends, television, the music industry, their teachers and coaches, their peers. Some teens are more influenced by godless tabloid stars than by their parents. As a God-called leader in the home, dare to influence your children in the things that matter most. By God's grace and wisdom, consciously plan to influence them to make choices, understand, and live by His standards and Word.

Will they listen? According to Religion News Service in March 2008, a survey of teens commissioned by the American Bible Society conducted by Weekly Reader Research overwhelmingly confirms that the number-one influence on teens in their religious activities and thoughts is their parents. Children tend to mirror their parents' behavior in attending church, praying, and reading the Bible. "Parents who attend church weekly tend to have teens who worship weekly, while 78 percent of parents who never attend worship services have teens who never attend. The same correlation applies to Bible reading and prayer habits." Parents who expressed a strong belief in raising children with religious or spiritual values had children who were significantly involved in a faith life. And do these youth realize they are following their parents' lead? The survey results reveal that 67.7 percent of 12- to 18-year-olds list their parents as the most important role models in society.

The altar is a sacred place for the family. Most members of the Body of Christ are married at the altar. We dedicate our children at the altar. We rededicate our vows to one another at the altar. One of our sons chose to propose to his wife at the church altar. But even when marriages begin at the altar, commitments will stray, and children will wander unless a continuing sacrifice is made at the altar of the heart and in the home.

A home altar provides opportunity for spiritual growth, instruction, and leadership. The home altar may be the dinner table, where children and parents feel comfortable to discuss the mundane and the eternal, the history test and the temper, the newest crush and the temptation of promiscuity. Despite the effort required in our rushed, over-scheduled families to get everyone at the dinner table together, godly parents look here for opportunities to lead through spiritual sensitivity, listening to the guidance of the Holy Spirit to take the conversation deeper or knowing when more talk means degenerating into what will be perceived as preachy and pushy.

A home altar may be at the bedside, where we pray nightly prayers with toddlers and grow into a comfortable lasting routine for conversations of spirit and eternal through teen years. A home altar may be at breakfast with a single Bible verse before kids dash out the door to catch the school bus. If we train up our children in the way they should go (Proverbs 22:6), we are not guaranteed they will walk that way all their lives. However, if the home altar is well established, a wayward child will know where to find it when he or she is ready to return.

The Gunter children are grown now with families of their own. We no longer have the privilege of daily prayers with them. But our extended family—our two sons, their wives, and our four grandchildren—began a tradition years ago. We all block out one week in our summer schedules for a family vacation together. The highlight of the week is our nightly devotional time. Each year we pick a theme, and each night a different couple or individual in the family presents the devotion—married couples, grandchildren, even our two youngest grandsons who have been teaming together, coming up with their own original devotion presentations since they were just little lads.

How our faith is strengthened each year as we see the spiritual growth occurring and hear the stories of God's faithfulness in their lives! One son testified to our family about the building program his local church had entered that year. He and his wife had made their financial pledge, trusting God to supply the resources for this aggressive commitment amount. Then, he shared, God spoke to him about increasing their pledge. How could they do this when their original pledge was already based on faith beyond what they had? In trust, he committed to the new amount God had revealed to him. How thrilled we were as he told about being called to the office of the company president the very next week! He was given an unexpected additional bonus—equal to the exact amount of the new pledge.

Last year our family's theme was defining moments in our lives. Granddaughter Lindsay shared how as a young teenager, her shyness kept her from making relationships with teens outside the church. At age 16, she prayed, asking God to increase her ability to make friends with nonbelievers. God gave her a promise to aid her confidence, and from that time on, she began to make friendships in her school. Today one of those unchurched teens she met in high school is a youth pastor's wife. Her husband, Jamin, shared how God revealed His direct will for him to attend a particular Christian university. No one from his family had attended that school, and Jamin had never even been on the campus. But when he and his dad arrived for their site visit, God brought peace and said, "This is the college for you." That led to many events he would never otherwise have experienced, including meeting Lindsay. We were all in tears at God's faithfulness to us at all stages of our lives.

Our oldest grandson, Trae, identified his junior year in college as a defining time of making decisions about his friends, surroundings, interests, career choices, and beliefs on a level that he had never considered before that time. Previously, he shared, he felt that he had little responsibility and was going through the motions of every aspect of his life. In the fall as he moved to a new community and chose a career, he felt he was truly thinking for himself. "This could be summed up as my first real acknowledgment and acceptance of responsibility," he said. We joined him in praise for these important steps in a journey of God's plan for his life.

Grandson Josh, age fifteen, shared about how God has led him in choosing to attend a new Christian school. Following the mindset of Robert Frost in his famous poem "The Road Not Taken," Josh's choice is like two roads diverging in a yellow wood, where "way leads on to way." He knows this decision will have lasting influence on his life from here forward. He shared the scripture that affirmed to him that this was God's will for this moment in his life.

Jacob, age 11, told us he has not yet experienced a real life-changing defining moment, but he knows that he will have some and has pledged before his family that whenever they happen, he will respond as God wants him to. This brought smiles all around.

These are precious moments for our family and treasured words for us to hear. However, they did not happen overnight. They are the product of now four generations of family altars and godly leadership within the home.

Does your home lack a "family altar" atmosphere? Is there lack of spiritual conversation or obvious discomfort when God-matters are mentioned? Is it too late to start? According to an old proverb, "The best time to plant a tree is 20 years ago. The second best time is now." Walt Disney said, "The way to get started is to quit talking and begin doing."

Today's hectic world needs holy leaders within the family. Our society's fast-paced, everyone-going-in-a-different-direction lifestyle will not stop for family prayer by accident. It will take purposeful leadership. Teaching our children the Bible, praying with them, and influencing them to personal prayer, devotional life, commitment, surrender, giving back to God, and growing in Him will take an on-purpose lifetime of leadership.

Dare to establish a spiritual relationship with your spouse that includes daily prayer and accountability. Take the lead. Where there have never been children or within the empty nest, husband and wife must bond together with spiritual ties that our me-first, consumer world cannot sever.

Dare to lead the way in putting God first in your family finances. Teach your family the biblical standards of tithing, both by example and by influence. As I (Gunter) was growing up, our family had nine boxes of tithing envelopes, one for each of us. Because my parents trained me in stewardship, I never struggled over tithing.

Dare to pray for your children. Let them know you are praying for them, and let them hear you call their names in prayer. Our greatest heritage is not in leaving earthly goods but in passing on a spiritual heritage through the generations.

Dare to control and then shift to influencing your children as they grow, even into adulthood. Teach them the Bible. Model and teach them personal integrity in all matters. We will never produce better citizens until we produce better children. By your teaching, your influence, and your witness, you may save a whole generation.

When the tsunami ripped across southeast Asia December 26, 2004, more than 287,000 people lost their lives. Complete villages were wiped out, some with no trace of human life remaining. Yet one tribe's population survived without harm. How? The Moken are sometimes called the sea gypsies. Spending six to nine months a year on their boats, they come ashore only periodically, living in primal temporary shelters. Because these primitive, animistic tribes know the sea as their home, on December 26 the elder leader recognized strange signs. Hastily he called for his entire tribe to hurry to higher ground in the nearby hillsides. How did he know? For perhaps centuries, generation after generation of the Moken has sat around a tribal campfire, passing on the story of how the sea once receded and then returned with unforgiving vengeance and complete destruction. Centuries later, one leader remembered and acted on the story he had heard around the fire. In so doing, he saved an entire race from extinction.

Testify to your family about your own spiritual challenges, growth, mistakes, and victories. Like the Israelites who crossed over the Jordan on dry ground, build those invisible but powerful rock towers that will point your spouse and your children to God's faithfulness. Choose to save your family. Dare to be a holy leader in your family through the power of the Holy Spirit. Start at home.

CHAPTER SIX

CONDUCT THE ORCHESTRA

"Peter and the Wolf" is a children's classic that combines story with instrumentation. Written by Sergei Prokofiev in 1936 for his son, the characters of the story are each represented by a single musical instrument playing an individual recurring theme. As the narrator begins the tale with the duck, we hear the oboe play his theme. When the bird, represented by the flute, and the duck get into an argument, the flute and oboe banter in a cacophony of duet. The sagely grandfather's words are expressed in the bassoon's deep notes, and the wolf merits three French horns. Rounded out by Peter/strings, the cat/clarinet, and the hunters, whose gunshots ring out with timpani and bass drum, "Peter and the Wolf" is one of the most recorded children's musical productions. To this day, many adults who first heard "Peter and the Wolf" on a fifth-grade field trip to the symphony still can hear in their minds the melody themes of each character's instrument. It sparked the first love that generated multitudes of season-ticket symphony-lovers.

However, those children-turned-music-aficionados quickly learned that "Peter and the Wolf" is one of the few musical compositions in which individual instruments are heard. That, of course, is one of the purposes of "Peter and the Wolf," to introduce children to the sounds of the bassoon and French horn, the oboe and timpani. Symphonies, however, are a blending of all the instruments, in which a single brass, string, woodwind, or percussion piece is rarely heard. Though the bassoon is always present at the Boston Pops, its bass notes add depth and richness to the orchestra without drawing attention to itself.

Symphony entered the English language through Old French from the Greek, and according to *Online Etymology Dictionary*, *symphonia*, means "harmony, concert." The word is formed from two roots, *syn-*, "together," and *phone*, "voice, sound." Since 1599 it came to mean "music in parts." In a true symphony we never hear the parts—we hear the "together voice" of music.

To work "in concert" with one another, to live harmoniously, to make our voices sound as one, we must strive for teamwork. The results are as beautiful as a symphony, but the process is rarely easy. It requires not only dedicated and talented players but also a skillful conductor.

Teamwork is contrary to everything within the individual. Since the fall of humanity, we have been about individual parts—my needs, my pursuits, my wants, my ambitions, my dreams, my desires, my goals. Me first. "I gotta be me." The location of the center of the earth is directly related to wherever I happen to be standing at the moment.

To paraphrase a cliché, there is no *I* in *symphony*.

Obviously athletics effectively illustrates leadership in teamwork. We sometimes conclude that because various players are gathered under one organization, because they wear the same uniform, because they have the same team name and coach, and because they work at the same time on the same playing field or court, they work as a team. But at any given time, a certain portion of the news on ESPN is about conflicts between management and players, contract disputes, free agents, and sports stars out of control.

Studies have shown that teams with the highest paid individual stars of the game do not necessarily win championships. When one or two members of the team are elevated in pay, egos rise correspondingly, thereby defeating team spirit, cooperation, and collaboration. Since the addition of professional players to the USA Olympic basketball team, superstar players' egos have run amuck. Coaches determined in 2008 to avoid having team captains at all. Even when the role of team captain called for one player to meet at center court with the referees and opposing team captain, USA coaches rotated this position from game to game. Run-and-gun ball-hogging basketball is no fun to watch, regardless the prowess of the stars, but drives down the soccer field in which the ball is strategically passed between six or seven players in an orchestrated weaving, resulting in a scored goal, brings the crowd to its feet every time.

Though *team* is the buzzword of almost every business today, it is rare to see it in practice. Some now consider it a dead term of corporate-speak. In its purest form, however, teamwork is the cooperative effort of people working together for a common goal without the interference of self-interests. Everything base about us wants to do our part of the whole individually, to be autonomous in our section of the goal, to work independently within an organization that has one mission. We work toward our own gratification, looking for our own rewards, accomplishing what makes us feel successful individually. We work independently of other so-called "team members" because they, in turn, are consumed with their own selfish interests, making us wary of any possibility of mutual trust.

Sadly, the church is sometimes the perfect laboratory to illustrate this individualism within a pseudo-team. As ministries grow larger, they also become more specialized. All have one common goal of making Christlike disciples, but in the process they segment off like pieces of a pie—a slice of children's ministries here, a slice of music ministries over there, a slice of evangelism elsewhere. Like radiologists, pediatricians, oncologists, and cardiologists all treating different parts of the body, the management of the individual parts, even by the most skillful specialists, will not necessarily produce holistic wellness in the patient. Who is determining how the treatment of cholesterol levels is interfacing with chemotherapy? Someone must be watching the potential for dangerous interactions of medications and treatments that are counterproductive to one another.

For years now, educators have promoted integrated learning. Lower math and reading skills resulting in lower test scores have sent creative leaders back to the drawing blackboard to find collaborative solutions. Interrelated disciplines offer students a more cohesive education as a science teacher, a history teacher, a math teacher, and a language arts teacher coordinate as a team on one unit or theme. Every subject's lesson plans—math, science, English—simultaneously revolve around a single topic, such as the Babylonian Empire or the "The Nutcracker" or the space program. Students see how various disciplines of reading, writing, art, math, and science are interwoven. As stand-alone skills suddenly make cohesive sense, interest increases and scores rise.

Though these integrated education methods have existed for decades, most teachers remain in their self-contained classrooms teaching their solitary subject where it has less relevance to the rest of the world. Those teachers, like many other leaders, are independent thinkers who cling tenaciously to their own opinions and methods and prefer autonomy in their own classrooms.

Whether in music or sports or medicine or education, holy leaders cannot ascribe to this system of multiple autonomous kingdoms under one roof pretending to be a team. From the beginning, we were created to be in relationship: "The LORD God said, 'It is not good for the man to be alone. I will make a helper suitable for him'" (Genesis 2:18).

We operate best within relationship because we are created in the image of God, who himself is a divine relationship of Father, Son, and Spirit.

Anyone who has seen me has seen the Father. How can you say, "Show us the Father"? Don't you believe that I am in the Father, and that the Father is in me? The words I say to you are not just my own. Rather, it is the Father, living in me, who is doing his work. Believe me when I say that I am in the Father and the Father is in me *(John 14:9-11)*.

I pray also for those who will believe in me through their message, that all of them may be one, Father, just as you are in me and I am in you. May they also be in us so that the world may believe that you have sent me. I have given them the glory that you gave me, that they may be one as we are one: I in them and you in me *(John 17:20-23)*.

Holy leaders recognize the difference between cooperation and collaboration. Cooperation is working together agreeably. Collaboration is working together aggressively. Working in the same environment, in close proximity, even within one company, church, or school does not necessarily produce teamwork. We can work cooperatively—amiably side by side—but we can work better collaboratively—in selfless tandem with one another under one vision—when we share ideas, coordinate plans, mesh the transitions from one person's responsibility to another, and intentionally communicate. We must lead our teams to be collaborators. Working together works.

Most hyphenated words beginning with *self-* are contrary to the Spirit-filled life. The holy leader must teach and model as a lifestyle an abandonment of self-interest, self-motivation, self-consumption, and self-gratification. Only through the power of the Holy Spirit can we die daily to our selfish interests in favor of God's direction for the greater good of the whole organization. It is not just pastors, missionaries, denominational leaders, and local church lay leaders who must consecrate themselves to selfless holy leadership. Regardless the venue, holy leaders as business owners, parents, principals, coaches, office supervisors, and community volunteers can best guide a group of individuals into a team. Whether the organization itself is holy or secular, the holy leader can set the tone through the power of the Holy Spirit for sacrificing self for the good of the whole.

Robert K. Greenleaf, considered the voice of servant leadership and applied ethics, said in *Servant Leadership: A Journey into the Nature of Legitimate Power and Greatness*, "The servant-leader *is* servant first. . . . It begins with the natural feeling that one wants to serve, to serve *first*. Then conscious choice brings one to aspire to lead. That person is sharply different from one who is *leader* first."

Though even secular leadership principles employ the word *servant*, holy leaders recognize this to mean not just one who serves but one who models himself after the Master Servant:

> He got up from the meal, took off his outer clothing, and wrapped a towel around his waist. After that, he poured water into a basin and began to wash his disciples' feet, drying them with the towel that was wrapped around him. He came to Simon Peter, who said to him, "Lord, are you going to wash my feet?" Jesus replied, "You do not realize now what I am doing, but later you will understand." "No," said Peter, "you shall never wash my feet." Jesus answered, "Unless I wash you, you have no part with me." "Then, Lord," Simon Peter replied, "not just my feet but my hands and my head as well!" . . . When he had finished washing their feet, he put on his clothes and returned to his place. "Do you understand what I have done for you?" he asked them. "You call me 'Teacher' and 'Lord,' and rightly so, for that is what I am. Now that I, your Lord and Teacher, have washed your feet, you also should wash one another's feet. I have set you an example that you should do as I have done for you" *(John 13:4-9, 12-14).*

Leadership is not a position or a right. It is not power or authority. Leadership is a responsibility. Paul encouraged Timothy that aspiring to leadership is noble. Holy leaders keep their eyes on the nobility of the true calling. Paul was not urging Timothy to seek the position. We learn from Jesus Christ that leading is not about titles, toys, or trinkets; it is about the towel of service—serving and influencing others. It is not enough simply to believe this. Intellectual assent and a proper understanding of selfless, Spirit-led relational leadership will be converted into behavior. A holy leader not only thinks according to the Spirit; he or she lives it in the day-to-day experiences of life.

We must build a team by clarifying the vision and living an exemplary lifestyle of selfless pursuit of that vision. The noble pursuit of the holy leader is to influence others to join in thinking, acting, and accomplishing a worthy mission.

Spirit-led relational leadership begins with love. A wise person told the Gunters early in their ministry, "Don't expect people to love you just because you are the pastor." Respect, love, and automatic attraction for following do not come with a title or position. Holy leaders seek to love before they seek to be loved.

Minnie Pearl, comedienne and Country Music Hall of Fame star, made her debut on WSM's Grand Ole Opry in Nashville on November 30, 1940. After her first performance, she broke into tears. George D. "Judge" Hay, founder of the Grand Ole Opry, put his arm around her and said, "Oh, Minnie, it's all right." "No," she said, "I failed! Tell me what to do. Tell me!" He replied, "Just love 'em, Minnie. Just love 'em." Many successful years later, Minnie Pearl said, "I remembered that for the rest of my life. My priority would be loving the people."

Love is foundational. The most successful teams are made of members who are intricately tied and devoted to one another. Holy leaders' love for followers must be authentic and pure in motive. That kind of love will fuel the passionate intensity of the heart and lead to relationships, the glue that holds the team together. If our primary motivation is to love people, we will desire to help them. Each team member helping the other means shared vision will be achieved.

Love never gives up. Love cares more for others than for self. Love doesn't want what it doesn't have. Love doesn't strut, Doesn't have a swelled head, Doesn't force itself on others, Isn't always "me first," Doesn't fly off the handle, Doesn't keep score of the sins of others, Doesn't revel when others grovel, Takes pleasure in the flowering of truth, Puts up with anything, Trusts God always, Always looks for the best, Never looks back, But keeps going to the end. Love never dies. . . . Trust steadily in God, hope unswervingly, love extravagantly. And the best of the three is love *(1 Corinthians 13:3-8, 13, TM).*

Living in relationship, true teams will exhibit respect, trust, reciprocity, and enjoyment. Team leaders put their energies into people because it is people—not programs or marketing or financial strategies—that move the mission. The Bible is replete with "one another's": be devoted to one another, honor one another, love one another, live in harmony with one another, instruct one another, greet one another, serve one another, be kind and compassionate to one another, submit to one another, encourage one another. Foundational to New Testament relationships is reciprocity. What you want, you give. What someone gives to you, you pass on.

No team can exist without reciprocal trust. Team members trust a leader who exhibits trust in them. Affirm them. Bless them. Speak well of them. Challenge them with increased levels of responsibilities as merited. Empower them with the amount of authority they need apart from you to accomplish their mission. Jesus gave the ultimate authority to His disciples: "He called his twelve disciples to him and gave them authority to drive out evil spirits and to heal every disease and sickness" *(Matthew 10:1).*

Trust your team members by delegating to them. Only the self-deluded leader thinks he or she can be everywhere and do everything. We connect and touch others through trusted representatives of ourselves. Let them in, align them, and let them out. Build energy and confidence by allowing them to network and partner with others. No great vision is achieved without risk. Jesus entrusted the entire future of His kingdom on earth to 11 "unlearned" followers:

> Then Jesus came to them and said, "All authority in heaven and on earth has been given to me. Therefore go and make disciples of all nations, baptizing them in the name of the Father and of the Son and of the Holy Spirit, and teaching them to obey everything I have commanded you" *(Matthew 28:18-20).*

Displaying trust in your followers builds confidence in their abilities to accomplish the task. In a culture of trust, they learn to trust others, to work collaboratively, and to create synergy within the team.

Holy leaders build teams who enjoy one another and enjoy their work. James A. Michener, Pulitzer Prize-winning novelist, said, "The master in the art of living makes little distinction between his work and his play, his labor and his leisure, his mind and his body, his information and his recreation, his love and his religion. He hardly knows which is which. He simply pursues his vision of excellence at whatever he does, leaving others to decide whether he is working or playing. To him he's always doing both." Let your team members catch you delighting in your work. It may be a contagious spirit.

Enjoy your team. Have fun together. Plan for enjoyable times away from work environment. Care for your team members. Express interest in their home life, their family members, and their personal concerns. Model for them a genuine, not manipulative, interest that will encourage them to reciprocate the same to their fellow team members. Paul told the believers at Thessalonica:

> You know we never used flattery, nor did we put on a mask to cover up greed—God is our witness. We were not looking for praise from men, not from you or anyone else. As apostles of Christ we could have been a burden to you, but we were gentle among you, like a mother caring for her little children. We loved you so much that we were delighted to share with you not only the gospel of God but our lives as well, because you had become so dear to us. . . . For you know that we dealt with each of you as a father deals with his own children, encouraging, comforting and urging you to live lives worthy of God, who calls you into his kingdom and glory *(1 Thessalonians 2:5-8, 11-12).*

Creating a team culture of love involves the leader's self-discipline. Sometimes only discipline holds us in a loving relationship when team members quibble and snipe, when they do not pull their fair share of the load, when they place self-interests ahead of the group, and when they temporarily lose sight of the team's goal. The children Paul loved like a mother were not always lovable. Real children display immature attitudes and behaviors that require loving correction and rebuke. This kind of love is not human, but it is possible for those leaders who are Spirit-led.

Caring about people requires basic courtesy. People too busy to return their phone calls are too busy for people, but Spirit-led relational leaders put people first. They foster a climate in which politeness is expected, people talk to one another kindly regardless the circumstance, apologies merited are given willingly, voice mail is never a regular diversion from people, and e-mails and correspondence are answered. Spirit-led relational leaders model being on time, honoring commitments, and keeping appointments. We regard people in every station of life as God's children, remembering that service is an attitude—not a department.

Robert Frost, United States poet laureate, said, "The most beautiful word in the world is the word *include*. The ugliest word in the world is *exclude*." Holy leaders take people in. We start with them where they are and journey with them. We share our dreams and vision with them. We invite them to be part of the mission.

Team members never segregate into *us* and *them*. Nothing will kill morale more quickly than physical barriers and verbal reminders that *you* are not part of *us*. If we are two separate groups, then which of us owns the vision—*us* or *them?* Why should I sacrifice my self-interest for the whole if I am not part of the whole?

People will be supportive of a mission in which they are included. Open communication with shared goals increases trust, respect, and participation. People gravitate toward those who love, accept, and value them. Love makes leading easier.

Spirit-led relational leaders build team by listening. Listen to God first. Spend time hearing His plan, His wisdom, and His vision. Store up in your heart what God communicates to you. As you listen to God, God can speak to others through you.

> The *good* man brings good things out of the good stored up in his heart . . . For out of the overflow of his heart his mouth speaks *(Luke 6:45).*

We must cultivate the art of carefully listening to others. "It's extremely important that we get our message out," said Condoleezza Rice, United States Secretary of State, "but it's also the case that we should not have a monologue with other people. It has to be a conversation, and you can't do that without exchanges and openness." Listening creates participation, a key ingredient of team. In participation, giving and taking, speaking and listening, we think *we, us,* and *our*—not *I, me,* and *mine.* No one of us has all the answers. In listening, we form synergy of ideas. We think together.

Sam Walton, founder of Wal-Mart Stores, set up a hot-line by which any employee anywhere could call headquarters in Bentonville, Arkansas. He invited conversation; he wanted to listen to others. If secular leaders are willing to take down the "Do Not Disturb" sign, how much more should holy leaders be an open door to good communication, quick to listen, slow to speak?

Certainly this does not mean we will always think alike or even that identical thinking is always desirable. General George Patton, Allied commander in World War II, said, "If everyone's thinking alike, then somebody isn't thinking." When we allow people to think and to speak without being intimidated, we foster a synergy of thought that helps accomplish the mission. Similarly, we must not be intimidated to hear what team members are thinking. As iterated by Winston Churchill, "Courage is what it takes to stand up and speak; courage is also what it takes to sit down and listen."

It is easier to lead people you love. It is easier to listen to people you love.

Spirit-led relational leaders never stop learning. The three years of Jesus' earthly ministry were filled with teaching His disciples, even after His resurrection. Holy leaders are lifelong learners, growing in the Word and in the guidance of the Spirit. The Spirit-filled lifestyle is stretching, leading us farther down the Christlike path today than we were yesterday. We must ask God to help us have a holy, healthy dissatisfaction with the way things are today as we advance toward the vision. As we daily relinquish self-serving goals, He will lead us farther into His preferred future and help us guide our team toward an ever-increasing vision of that future.

As we discover more about His preferred future, we need to organize our teams most effectively for action. Flute players belong in the woodwinds, not the percussion section. Lightweight, fast runners should be positioned as wide receivers, not on the line. Sanguines belong out front with the public, not in the accounting department. Christopher Robin told Winnie the Pooh, "'Organizing' is what you do before you do something, so that when you do it it's not all mixed up."

To advance towards God's preferred future, we must learn more about ourselves and our team members. To place them in the most strategic positions of the team, we must know their temperaments, strengths, and weaknesses. And we must dare to delve for additional insight about ourselves.

Temperament surveys and strengths finder inventories have become popular tools for organizational effectiveness. But we cannot use these to the neglect of the Holy Spirit, nor can we use them as crutches for weaknesses or deficiencies by saying, "That's just who I am. Get used to it." Suddenly, then, we are back to the "I gotta be me" syndrome.

However, used in the context of a Spirit-guided relational team, knowing the strengths and weaknesses of ourselves and our team members is beneficial. Each year in our office team retreat (Dr. Gunter's), we focused on leadership development. In preparation for one retreat, we all read *Now, Discover Your Strengths,* by Marcus Buckingham and Donald O. Clifton. We completed a personal inventory profile to identify our individual strengths and weaknesses. In the retreat, we began to share with fellow team members what we had learned about ourselves.

My strength areas were:

Learning—a great desire to acquire knowledge and constantly improve

Responsibility—taking psychological ownership for one's beliefs and actions

Belief—firm adherence to core values

Activation—turning thoughts into action

But right at the top of my list of strengths was:

Ideation—having new ideas and finding new and creative methods of achieving the mission

"Oh," one of my staff said immediately, "*now* we understand. You come in with these new projects and new ideas because that's one of your natural strengths." Suddenly they understood that I was not just dreaming up new tasks for them; I was consumed with a God-implanted passion for finding creative new ways to challenge other people to get involved in the mission.

We shared with one another, understanding the strengths and weaknesses of each team member. We discovered a cello player was misplaced in the trumpet section. We found one member's strengths could augment another's weakness and paired them for greater effectiveness to complement one another. We found common strengths with which certain team members could begin new collaboration of efforts.

A tourist once asked a guide, "Were any famous leaders born in this city?" The guide replied, "No, just babies." We are all tempted with pride in our strengths, but no one has a blank "Weaknesses" column. No one is born with all it takes to be an effective holy leader. We must recognize rather than disregard our weaknesses and learn to manage rather than excuse them.

We are shaped by God-given strengths, talents, skills, and temperaments. Because we are God's children by grace, we must be willing to sharpen those skills and maximize our strengths. We must submit to self-discipline. Thomas Huxley, a 19th century biologist, had this to say about discipline: "Perhaps the most valuable result of all education is the ability to make yourself do the thing you have to do, when it ought to be done, whether you like it or not; it is the first lesson that ought to be learned; and however early a man's training begins, it is probably the last lesson that he learns thoroughly." It takes discipline to be better at what we naturally do well.

Commit to being a lifelong learner, regardless the success you achieve or the level you reach. We are on a continuing journey. Read, study, pay attention to details. Seek to improve yourself. Add value to your team by being more resourceful.

Be humble enough to learn from your team members. Remain teachable, and cultivate a culture of learning. Be an agent of change. Adapt without compromising the mission. Create new methods without abandoning the principles. It is better to prepare than repair. Sam Walton never grew tired of learning: "I probably have traveled and walked into more variety stores than anybody in America. I am just trying to get ideas, any kind of ideas that will help our company. Most of us don't invent ideas. We take the best ideas from someone else."

People generally will reach the bar wherever we set it. Is your team's bar too low? If we think we're on a dead-end street, we are. If we think nothing will happen, our anticipation will be realized. If we think our team members are not going to work as a team, they won't. Follow Mark Twain's advice and set the standard high: "Twenty years from now you will be more disappointed by the things that you didn't do than by the ones you did do. So throw off the bowlines. Sail away from the safe harbor. Catch the trade winds in your sails. Explore. Dream. Discover."

The Boston Pops Orchestra is arguably one of the best known orchestras in the world. Yet few people know that it was founded in 1885 as a "second-string" set of players. Pops or festival orchestras were generally formed of principal players who served as the assistant or associate players of the parent organization. In this case, the members of the Boston Pops were the Boston Symphony Orchestra minus the first-chair players.

The Boston Pops did not have its own permanent conductor until 1930, when Arthur Fiedler began his 50-year tenure there. Dissatisfied with the reputation of classical music as being only for an elite upper class, Fiedler wanted to bring classical music to a wider, more common audience. He instituted a series of unconventional changes, including free concerts in a public park along the Charles River. His repertoire included not only classical pieces but also popular music. In doing so, he created a new niche in the music world—a popularization of classical music. If you can hear in your mind the strains of "Sleigh Ride" or orchestral renditions of the greatest hits of the Beatles, you're probably hearing the Boston Pops. You can thank Arthur Fiedler for that melody in your head.

A skillful conductor with a vision can take a group of second-stringers and form them into the only orchestra with a regularly televised performance on PBS, "Evening at the Pops."

Holy leaders are about a mission they cannot accomplish alone. It takes teamwork. Pick up the baton. The instruments are tuning up.

CHAPTER SEVEN

PAY IT FORWARD

A woman standing on a curb grabs the back of the jacket of the pizza delivery boy beside her just before he steps into the path of an oncoming car. A man watching this is inspired to help a mother carry a baby stroller off the bus. A man sitting at the bus stop watching this is inspired to help a coworker in the kitchen lift a heavy bowl from a high shelf. A cook watching this is inspired as she walks past two boys playing basketball to kick their stray ball back to them to prevent it from rolling into the street. A man driving by watching this is inspired to pull a bulky suitcase off the airport conveyor belt for an elderly man. The pattern continues: someone opens the hotel door for a bellman laden with luggage; a man returns money from a public laundry washing machine to the person who just removed his clothes; someone gives up her seat on the bus; another moves an item about to trip someone—each person doing a kind deed because he or she saw someone else do one. It continues to a woman inspired by seeing someone plug the parking meter for a person who has no coins. Her act of kindness? She's the one who pulls the pizza delivery boy back from impending danger. It's a circle. The Liberty Mutual Insurance television commercial is clear: Good deeds beget good deeds beget good deeds.

Pay It Forward, a book by Catherine Ryan Hyde, was made into a movie in 2000. A teacher seeks to inspire his middle school students by giving them a unique assignment: Think of an idea that could change the world, and put it into action. The 12-year-old hero of the story describes his idea this way: "You see, I do something real good for three people. And then when they ask how they can pay it back, I say they have to pay it forward—to three more people each. So nine people get helped. Then those people have to do 27. Then it sort of spreads out. See?" The numbers increase exponentially requiring a calculator: 81, 243, 729, 2,187. The idea is an action plan set in a fiction story, but it has been given real life through the Pay It Forward Foundation, which encourages students to create acts of kindness and provides grants and materials to make them reality. The message is clear: Good deeds beget good deeds beget good deeds.

Our calling is clear: Holy leaders beget holy leaders beget holy leaders.

> What you have heard from me through many witnesses entrust to faithful people who will be able to teach others as well *(2 Timothy 2:2, NRSV).*

Teach means primarily today "to impart knowledge." *Online Etymology Dictionary* tells us that it originated from the Old English *tæcan*, which meant not only to impart wisdom but also "to show, to point out" and that it carried connotations of warning, showing the way, and signs. *Teacher* emerged in English as "one who teaches." Interestingly, the same word had been used earlier to mean index finger. Those who teach are pointing the way.

Often the people who have the most knowledge to impart and who appear to be the most worthy to point the way to others tend to be the busiest people. They are the "faithful people who will be able to teach others." It is often these busiest people who should be teaching the classes, writing the books, conducting the seminars, and mentoring the protégés. Yet these are the very people who say, "My life is too hectic and my schedule too slammed to add one more responsibility." Almost all holy leaders live in a hectic world.

Paige Arnof-Fenn, founder and CEO of the strategic marketing consulting firm Mavens and Moguls, said in "Leaving a Legacy": "I've been so busy building my business that I didn't make the time to think about the bigger issues like who'll keep my dreams alive without me here."

If the busiest people do not mentor others, then to whom is the responsibility left? Do we really want just anyone who has ample time on his or her hands mentoring the next generation of leaders?

The level of customer service we experience today is directly related to the degree of training that employees are receiving from qualified leaders. Our cable and Internet provider has a monopoly on our geographical area. Because they know we have no alternative, their leadership has created a culture of slipshod training replicated in performance all the way down the chain of command. Their ineptitude is no secret even to themselves, evident through their obviously contrived strategies for dealing with person after person who is dissatisfied, frustrated, or downright angry. Unprompted, the telephone representatives automatically insert into their conversation about every third sentence: "I do understand. . . . We apologize for that. . . . We apologize for your inconvenience. . . . I'm sorry about that." This in itself is a constant reminder that they are fully aware of their deficiencies in meeting their customers' needs. Yet there is no improvement coming where the bottom line is profitable and leaders are too busy to care.

The same can be true of a church, a restaurant, a hotel, a classroom, or any business. However, most of these do not enjoy a monopoly and a secure bottom line. Where there is choice, customers walk away. Parents choose magnet or charter schools. Consumer-minded Christians change churches. Leaders must be intent on excellence and committed to propagating their philosophy to everyone in the organization. Where overall operations are sloppy and attitudes nonchalant, inspiration to be the best either does not exist in the top management or is not being taught by leaders too busy to point the way to excellence.

If we are holy leaders today, passionate about excellence in our homes, churches, schools, and businesses, it is because someone invested time and energy in us. The culture of self-made, pull-yourself-up-by-your-own-bootstraps thinking is self-deluded. We did not get here on our own. Regardless our amount of work and study, we did not teach ourselves all that we know. We are not self-achievers. Isaac Newton, 17th-century scientist considered by many the greatest in history, wrote in a letter, "If I have seen further it is by standing on ye shoulders of Giants." We are all standing on someone's shoulders.

Within the Christian world today, mentoring may be one of the most neglected spiritual disciplines of all. Mentoring requires *time*, that illusive quality that many holy leaders cannot accumulate, do not have in excess, will not part with, and constantly overstuff. Mentoring requires discipline to *let go* in order to *take on*.

Hectic leaders are task-oriented. We make our "to do" list and rush through the day to achieve our goal of having nothing left to roll over to tomorrow's list. Some so delight in crossing through items that they will write down tasks *after* they have done them for the pure joy of marking them off.

In contrast, holy leaders are people-oriented. As Leonard Sweet in his book *11 Indispensable Relationships You Can't Be Without* wrote, "Have you ever considered that your Sistine Chapel might not be a place or a project but a person?" What thing are you doing now that you could give up in order to take on a person instead?

Make no mistake: holy leaders are no less busy than hectic leaders. They have equal numbers of to-do tasks waiting. But those led by the Spirit put people first because God himself is people-oriented, not task-oriented.

Successful leaders have an innate desire to leave behind a legacy not only of their work but also of themselves invested in others. Though their lifetimes never overlapped, from Socrates (469–399 B.C.) to Alexander the Great (356–323 B.C.), the chain of paying it forward is unbroken:

- Socrates, a Greek classical philosopher credited as one of the founders of Western philosophy, mentored Plato, considered the world's first systematic philosopher and founder of the Academy in Athens, the first institution of higher learning in the Western world.

- Plato in turn mentored Aristotle, whose teachings on philosophy and a wide range of topics influenced Western thought and are still taught today.
- Aristotle's student was Alexander the Great, king of Macedon and conqueror of much of Asia.

Sigmund Freud, founder of psychoanalysis, mentored Carl Jung, founder of analytical psychology. Anne Sullivan brought the gift of communication to Helen Keller, author and lecturer, blind and deaf since the age of two. Sherwood Anderson, early 20th-century American author, critiqued the work of Ernest Hemingway, who became arguably the greatest American writer of his generation. Anderson also mentored William Faulkner, Thomas Wolfe, William Saroyan, John Steinbeck, and other writers, several of whom earned the Nobel and Pulitzer prizes for literature.

A qualified leader imparts to the inexperienced not only wisdom, skill, and knowledge but also a sense of security, a safety net, and a new confidence. Knowing that someone believes in them enough to invest in them brings new hope. Shoulders to stand on provide new vistas never before imagined.

If the world sees the importance of passing on knowledge and experience in philosophy, government, literature, and music, to name just a few topics, how much more should holy leaders invest time, energy, and trust to replicate themselves in other holy leaders? Moses poured himself into Joshua; Elijah took Elisha as a protégé; Paul mentored Timothy.

It was God's blessing to me that Louise Robinson Chapman chose to invest herself in me. As an ordained minister, Dr. Chapman served as a missionary to Africa from 1920 until 1942.

In Endzingeni, Swaziland, she superintended the Girls' Training School where she cared for literally hundreds of young women, teaching them in English and Zulu, leading their Bible studies, and training them in practical skills. Some of these women became evangelists, Bible teachers, and preachers' wives. She later shared her skills among the men, helping to prepare pastors at the Men's Training School. At the same time, she served as pastor of the local church at different periods and supervised about 15 preaching posts nearby. In "Wesleyan Holiness Women Clergy," Stan Ingersol said of Chapman, "Evangelism was her favorite task. 'Africa is all I see,' she wrote, 'and her people are, to me, the most beautiful of all the tribes of earth.'"

While home on furlough, she was prevented by world war from returning to her beloved Africa and became president of the global missions organization of the Church of the Nazarene from 1948 to 1964, throwing all her energies and creativity into supporting missions around the world. As told by Howard Culbertson in *Mission to the World*, this woman of faith, tenacity, and prayer was known for her philosophy "If you don't like it, change it!"

No wonder I was privileged that she chose to invest in me. She modeled all the characteristics I wanted to display in my life of service to God. She taught me to be a person of prayer. In advanced age, when Dr. Chapman was asked to give a challenge to her denomination at their general missions convention where thousands of people would be in attendance, she responded, "Let me pray about it." While most leaders seek a platform, she wanted to be sure this invitation was from God rather than from human leaders. After days of prayer she said, "God could have asked 1,000 people to do this, but He has asked me, so I will do the best I can."

I never had the slightest hesitation that I could go to her with any question, any prayer request, any burden and she would respond in Christlike love that would mold me for life. She taught me principles of leadership through her words and her lifestyle. She encouraged me, loved me, counseled me, challenged me, prayed for me, and blessed me. Though she lived to be 100 years old, she was married only five of those years and had no children. Yet she called me her daughter and herself my mother.

"My dear daughter, Nina," she once wrote to me, "God's hand is on you. He will continue to bless your efforts. I pray for you every day. With much love, your mother, Louise."

Whose shoulders are you standing on? Who is standing on your shoulders? We must invest in others, perpetuate leadership, reproducing and multiplying ourselves. We must pray, encourage, lift, correct, and hold accountable.

The process is long. Patience and longsuffering are prerequuisites. We are not turning out cupcakes; we are molding lives. Sometimes we will not see the results for many years or perhaps never in our lifetimes.

Idaho farmers prepare the soil for two to three years before potatoes are ever planted. The soil must be worked deeply to break up any hard portions. All stones, rocks, and debris must be removed. The farmers must mix in straw, compost, and other loose materials into the soil three to six inches deep over acres and acres of land. They must till and turn the soil, giving it time to develop into a rich muck. After no crops for two to three years, they are prepared to plant the potato tubers.

Then they fertilize every two to four weeks. As the plants grow, farmers must regularly bring in additional soil to mound around the plants so that the tubers or potatoes are never exposed to sunlight. They cover the soil around the plants with compost, mulch, or plastic. After years of preparing the soil, harvest comes.

In leadership development, no time spent cultivating is wasted. Relationships must be built. Trust must be established that comes only through the test of time. Patterns of behavior and responsibility must be modeled that merit the attention of a protégé. What are you doing now that would entice someone to spend more time with you, to adopt your style, or to learn from your character?

Leaders are not manufactured wholesale. They are produced one by one. Group dynamics, teamwork, and synergy all contribute to the growth of a fledging leader, but intensive personal attention from one teacher to one learner provides opportunities for questions, interaction, and emulation. Socrates could have taught all who gathered at the Athens forum, but he chose to pour himself into Plato in a concerted effort to mentor the next generation.

Every generation has the responsibility to pass on the message and the mission to the next generation, just as pure and holy as it was handed to us. Those leaders before us drew out the best in us, and we must do so for those who follow.

With the constant threats Paul lived under, he knew a long lifespan was not guaranteed to him. He had been beaten, shipwrecked, and imprisoned. At one point more than 40 men plotted his death and "bound themselves with an oath not to eat or drink until they had killed Paul" (Acts 23:12-13).

> I am already being poured out like a drink offering, and
> the time has come for my departure *(2 Timothy 4:6).*

Paul sensed not just a need but an *urgent* need to replicate himself in Timothy so that the leadership in the Church would not depend on himself or any other single person.

How gratifying it must be to the leader who returns from a conference or a vacation to accolades of "Things just aren't the same around here without you." "No one can fill your shoes." "Thank goodness you're back, and don't leave again anytime soon." Affirmations feel good, but holy leaders put the greater good above their own good feelings. Every great leader knows that no successful organization revolves for long around just one person.

In order to build the next generation of leadership, Paul allowed Timothy to participate in the ministry. Timothy was no onlooker, sideline observer, or intern. Paul involved him in the fray, from city to city, allowing him to join in the preaching. Paul wanted Timothy to learn not only by watching and listening to him but by actual on-the-job, hands-on training. He wanted Timothy to experience the full job description first-hand—even the suffering:

> Join with me in suffering for the gospel, by the power
> of God, who has saved us and called us to a holy life—not
> because of anything we have done but because of his own
> purpose and grace *(2 Timothy 1:8-9).*

He trusted Timothy out of his sight. Timothy was a frequent emissary for Paul, traveling to other churches and cities to take the message and to minister on his own:

For this reason I am sending to you Timothy, my son whom I love, who is faithful in the Lord. He will remind you of my way of life in Christ Jesus, which agrees with what I teach everywhere in every church *(1 Corinthians 4:17)*.

However, many leaders are willing to allow their protégés to come just so far. Though they have committed their efforts and time to this process, they have not yet died to their ability to control. In short, their egos lead their protégés to a brick wall.

You can watch me, Ego says.

You can listen to me.

You can admire me and even emulate me.

But you cannot participate with me.

The problem that prevents many hectic leaders from replicating themselves in participatory leadership is perfectionism. With time constraints and high expectations, they "teach the class" but never "open the laboratory." Most unfortunately, some holy leaders can say a reluctant "Me too" here.

After all, Ego rationalizes, *my insistence on excellence is the major fuel that propelled me to where I am today in this demanding role of leadership.*

Delegation of tasks risks that someone will not meet our expectations, will not achieve our level of excellence, and ultimately will detract from our performance.

No one, Ego believes, *regardless the level of training—even training from me—will be able to do this task to my standards. It is safer, faster, and easier to do the job myself than to model, teach, and trust someone else to do it.*

From this arrogant self-assurance that leads to exclusivity, holy leaders must repent.

Interns must be allowed off the bench and on the playing field. Protégés must get in the fray, get their hands dirty, experiment with their dreams, and try their skills. And, yes, they must make their mistakes. Which of us did not?

When I was 24 years of age, my husband and I, just out of seminary, accepted the pastorate of our first church, a congregation in South Carolina. We had been there only a short time when I was appointed to be a member of the district Nazarene Missions International council, the denomination's missions support organization. I had no idea what this role would involve. I did not know anything about what I would be asked to do. Truthfully, I hardly knew what the organization's acronym meant. I vividly recall walking into that first council meeting. I was young, inexperienced, and unknowledgeable. Though men had been incorporated into membership 10 years earlier, the organization was still operated mostly by women. And as strange as it may seem today, those 40- and 50-some-year-old women looked so old to me. *What am I doing here? Should I have accepted this position? Will I embarrass myself with my ignorance?*

It did not take long for those feelings to vanish. Those women took me in, seeing the opportunity to translate a passion for missions to the next generation. I began to feel their warmth. They gave me responsibility and taught me how to accomplish it. I watched them lead. I heard their dreams. I caught their vision. I saw the biblical base for missions. Their passion became mine. I thank them to this day for including me, teaching me, mentoring me, delegating to me, and encouraging me.

Holy leaders must not only consent to invest themselves in others. We must not only sacrifice our time and our willingness to allow participation within leadership. We must do all this, but we must do it *passionately*. We must be consumed with a passion to perpetuate leadership with righteous motivations.

Before you begin, check yourself:

_____ Do I understand that Christ is trusting me with one of His children for training and molding?

_____ Do I have any self-serving, carnal, or inauthentic motives for investing in this person?

_____ Am I mentoring this person for a sense of my own power, prestige, or ego?

_____ Am I spending time with this person because it feeds my sense of importance?

_____ Am I willing to delegate to this person tasks that I think only I can perform?

_____ Am I submitting myself to the Lordship of Jesus Christ to model holy leadership and not just the best corporate leadership practices?

_____ Do I see this person as a privilege, not as a task or a project?

_____ Am I doing this because I want to perpetuate holy leadership in this person's home, church, office, and career?

_____ Am I truly passionate about pouring not just my ideas and my methods but myself into this person?

When your motivations are right, your ego checked, and your schedule sacrificed, ask the Holy Spirit to guide you to the person of His choosing. Prayerfully consider who God might already be sending to your doorstep. To whom do you feel a supernatural drawing? In whom do you believe your influence could have impact for holy purposes?

Recognize that all fledgling leaders are not candidates for discipling. Some do not realize their need for personal growth. Others will not commit to the discipline. Not everyone who starts finishes—"Do your best to come to me quickly, for Demas, because he loved this world, has deserted me and has gone to Thessalonica" (2 Timothy 4:9-10).

Instead, invest yourself in those like Timothy who seek instruction, take constructive criticism, desire to be coached, recognize that they do not already know all the answers, follow through with assignments, and face a challenge.

Holy leaders build a godly unity with their protégés. Let them into your lives. Share your personal experiences with them. Allow them to see beyond your business practices to your heart. Set regular times for meeting and maintain consistency. Set common goals. Share the ownership of this relationship. Unite in discipleship, partnership, and mutual aspirations.

Holy leaders seek to nurture their protégés. Recognize that individuals come from different backgrounds and arrive at the partnership in varying degrees of readiness. This is a process, not a project. Walk with them on their journey. Determine your ground zero and where to start. Set the pace according to the individual. Spend time cultivating and nurturing at whatever level is needed. Do not feed meat to babies.

I gave you milk, not solid food, for you were not yet ready for it. Indeed, you are still not ready *(1 Corinthians 3:2).*

Holy leaders find innovative ways to disciple their protégés. Create a vision and passionately share it. Teach them not only what you were taught but what you are learning on your current journey. Recommend the books you are reading. Read them together and discuss what you gleaned from them. Share your mistakes with those who are spiritually mature enough to handle this knowledge. Admit when you do not know the answer. Be open to their discoveries. Be humble enough to learn from your student.

Holy leaders display trust in their protégés. Your belief in them will foster new levels of their self-confidence. Release positions of leadership and responsibility to them. Choose to fertilize, not sterilize.

I give you this charge: Preach the Word; be prepared in season and out of season; correct, rebuke and encourage— with great patience and careful instruction *(2 Timothy 4:1-2).*

Holy leaders act on their passion to leave a legacy. Sometimes we see the results in the generations of our own family. Sometimes we see someone walking in our footprints in our school, our office, or our pastoral staff. But will we always see the results? We stood on someone's shoulders, but sometimes we sense no one standing on ours.

Not long ago I traveled to a country where only a set number of state-approved Christian churches exist but where hundreds of thousands of Christians are gathering regularly in underground house churches. I came as a guest of the government and was escorted by officials who treated me kindly and with respect but never left me and those traveling with me. I spoke in one of the approved churches on a Sunday morning to a packed sanctuary of 700 people, including my ever-present government host.

I knew that in this very province our church had once had a thriving ministry from the 1920s until the early 1940s. Missionaries operated a Bible college, a hospital, and vibrant evangelistic thrusts here. But they had been forced to leave during the war, the government had confiscated the properties, and the Bible college and hospital were shut down.

Had the life investment of two decades paid off? Seventy years later, was it inconceivable that remnants might yet be found among a new generation?

In preparation for my travels, I had learned that a nondenominational residential seminary has been allowed to exist in this province now. School administrators had extended an invitation for me to speak, and the government had approved me to go.

I spent four of the most memorable hours of my life with those students, teaching and interacting with them. As we shared fellowship over hot tea and cookies, the elderly matron of the school introduced me to her three granddaughters, all of whom are students at this seminary, preparing for the ministry. She brought out a 14 x 17-inch sepia photograph. Pictured there were the members of the 1941 graduation class—the last class of our Bible college. Proudly she pointed to one man. "This one," she said, "was my father. He was an evangelist."

The missionaries had gone, the property had changed hands, but those trained in the school remained true. They went underground; they went from house to house; they shared the gospel one-on-one. "We know who we are," she said. "We have not forgotten." Amazingly, later in my travels, another minister for several government-approved churches showed me the same

1941 photo and identified his grandfather, also a member of the Bible school's last graduating class.

They are all standing on the shoulders of giants. The lineage from banished Bible college teachers to the school matron's father had been passed to her, to her children, and to her grandchildren. His three great-granddaughters, the fourth generation, are now preparing for ministry and are already traveling on weekends to preach and conduct Bible studies.

They are not alone. Today they report that there are about 200,000 Christian believers in just two provinces with their roots in our ministries that "concluded" there almost 70 years ago!

Those forced to leave, never to return, had worked with confidence, trusting God that their investment in the lives of their student leaders would one day pay divine dividends in generation after generation of new leaders whom they would never meet on this earth. They would not be disappointed.

May the favor of the Lord our God rest upon us;
establish the work of our hands for us—
yes, establish the work of our hands *(Psalm 90:17).*

Holy leaders beget holy leaders beget holy leaders. It is the divine multiplication plan. Is it time for you to hoist someone up on your shoulders?

CHAPTER EIGHT

REMEMBER JESUS

As Nels Ferre grew up in Scandinavia, almost everyone around him took note that he was not an average boy. Like those who have been ordained from the day of conception, it seemed unmistakably apparent that God had invested in him special qualities that marked him as different from other children in his school. Raised by a godly mother who recognized an increased level of responsibility for the careful management of God's gifts to her son, Nels grew up knowing God and accepting Jesus Christ as his personal Savior. But there was more. Nels had an innate brilliance that was evident to all. In fact, it was other members of the community who went to his mother with the suggestion that such a precocious child should be nurtured and educated in a manner that was not possible in his home town. "We'd like him to go to America and study at the finest institutions," they said and promised some resources to make it possible. Though she was devoted to God and aware of the investment others were willing to make in her son, how could she part with him at the tender age of 12, knowing she might never see him again?

When the plans were made and the day dawned when he would leave home, his mother took young Nels to the train station for the first part of a long journey that would take him into a lifetime of theological leadership. He watched as his mother purchased his ticket and arranged for his meager luggage. As she guided her adolescent son into the unknown future, she kissed him dearly and sent him up the train steps. "When you get on the train, try to find a seat by the window," she told him. "I'll be standing here, and we can see one another." He followed her instructions and in a moment was peering out the window at his mother standing alone on the platform. As they made eye contact for the last time, a parting message came to her mind, simple yet life-changing. She cupped her hands to her mouth and said to her son, "Remember Jesus." The engines fired and the train cars groaned as their heavy wheels responded. The train began inching away. Muffled by the noise of the ever-increasing movement of the train, he could no longer hear her voice, but he read the message on her lips as she continued to repeat, "Remember Jesus! Remember Jesus!" A lifetime of study and leadership later, when theologian, teacher, and author Nels Ferre was living his last days, he was asked, "What message helped you stay focused on the mission God gave you so long ago?" It was a simple, yet profound message, he said, one delivered by his mother to a 12-year-old boy going away to face the unknown, silently mouthed but ingrained in his heart forever: "Remember Jesus."

When life comes at us with blurring speed, when demands are greater than the store of energy or the hands on the clock, when God and family are overrun by tyrannical quotas to be met, papers to be graded, diapers to be changed, meetings to be chaired, or sermons to be written—the single focus that will bring order out of chaos is "Remember Jesus."

> Therefore, holy brothers, who share in the heavenly calling, fix your thoughts on Jesus, the apostle and high priest whom we confess *(Hebrews 3:1)*.

Our focus on Him is the sole way to prioritize among the distractions of this hectic world into which He calls us to serve as holy leaders. Only a single-minded concentration on the One who called us to leadership will enable us to serve God faithfully in our assigned roles. Clergy or laity, our calling to leadership is divine, and we must look to the divine Giver of the calling for grace, mercy, strength, and guidance.

Yet the very nature of leadership is entangled with self-made snares. Leadership brings with it accoutrements of authority, power, control, privilege, and perks that threaten to lull us into a false sense of autonomy and hollow arrogance. The more followers one has, the more temptation to perceive oneself as privileged, exempt, invincible, and beyond accountability. Powerful figures have toppled not from conquering armies but from internal disintegration of morals and ethics and a haughty spirit fueled by Satan that infects the organization from within, causing it to decay.

Conrad Black was once considered the third biggest newspaper magnate in the world. As chairman of Hollinger International, he built a media business that spanned three continents, including the *Chicago Sun Times*, *Jerusalem Post*, *Daily Telegraph* (United Kingdom), *National Post* (Canada), and hundreds of community newspapers in North America. In "Black Narcissi," columnist Dominic Rushe called Black "intelligent, belligerent and pompous." He made friends with powerful political figures such as Henry Kissinger and Margaret Thatcher and counted many more as acquaintances. But financial irregularities, allegedly to fund his lush lifestyle, and what Rushe called "a Maxwellian disregard for the rules" resulted in a 2007 conviction in a United States federal court and a sentence of 78 months in prison. Most telling are Rushe's words: "He appeared to believe in his own infallibility, but as a historian he should have known every empire designs its own demise, including his own."[1]

The Conrad Black path is well traveled by a much longer list than these leaders deluded by their own power:

Imelda Marcos of the Philippines, billionaire, is remembered most for the 2,700 pairs of shoes she left behind in one of her palaces as she and her husband fled the uprising to their corrupt dictatorship.

Michael Vick, former quarterback of the Atlanta Falcons, was convicted of illegal dog fighting and sentenced to the United States Penitentiary in Leavenworth, Kansas.

John Edwards had this to say about lying about his extra-marital affair during his campaign for president of the United States: "I went from being a senator, a young senator to being considered for vice-president, running for president, being a vice-presidential candidate and becoming a national public figure—all of which fed a self-focus, an egotism, a narcissism that leads you to believe that you can do whatever you want. You're invincible. And there will be no consequences."[2]

Surely any person who has tasted God's goodness, experienced His forgiveness, and embraced Him in worship could not consider being unfaithful to Him. Yet we can all think of those who have strayed. People called by God to holy leadership, equipped by the power of the Holy Spirit, who have failed by their own delusion of self-success run from 20th-century televangelists all the way back to King Saul.

"What have you done?" asked Samuel. Saul replied, "When I saw that the men were scattering, and that you did not come at the set time, and that the Philistines were assembling at Micmash, I thought, 'Now the Philistines will come down against me at Gilgal, and I have not sought the LORD's favor.' So I felt compelled to offer the burnt offering." "You acted foolishly," Samuel said. "You have not kept the command the LORD your God gave you; if you had, he would have established your kingdom over Israel for all time. But now your kingdom will not endure; the LORD has sought out a man after his own heart and appointed him leader of his people, because you have not kept the LORD's command" *(1 Samuel 13:11-14)*.

Where hectic schedules and pressuring demands collide with raw power, leaders without the guidance of the Holy Spirit are left to their own cunning and the resulting corruption. Solomon admonished all whom God calls to be holy leaders: "Above all else, guard your heart, for it is the wellspring of life" (Proverbs 4:23).

God is the divine discerner of our thoughts. Nothing is hidden from Him: "Yet you know me, O LORD; you see me and test my thoughts about you" (Jeremiah 12:3).

Holy leaders understand the ever-present, all-knowing power of the omniscient God. In wisdom, they run *to* His inspection rather than *away* from it. They seek God's piercing eyes into their motives, their plans, their innermost hidden intentions. They request the investigating finger of God to point out character flaws, abuse of power, and self-delusion.

God, investigate my life; get all the facts firsthand. I'm an open book to you; even from a distance, you know what I'm thinking. You know when I leave and when I get back; I'm never out of your sight. You know everything I'm going to say before I start the first sentence. I look behind me and you're there, then up ahead and you're there, too—your reassuring presence, coming and going. This is too much, too wonderful—I can't take it all in! Is there anyplace I can go to avoid your Spirit? to be out of your sight? . . . Investigate my life, O God, find out everything about me; Cross-examine and test me, get a clear picture of what I'm about; See for yourself whether I've done anything wrong—then guide me on the road to eternal life *(Psalm 139:1-7, 23-24, TM)*.

A serious problem holy leaders encounter in secular and even Christian leadership seminars, books, and lectures is that the best leadership practices tainted with the least bit of self-serving motivation go awry. Take, for example, the principle of affirmation. Some leadership experts advise giving compliments to members of your team within the first three minutes of a conversation or meeting. Encouraging others is a principle of good leadership. Certainly the Bible affirms this among the Body of Christ:

Encourage one another and build each other up, just as in fact you are doing *(1 Thessalonians 5:11).*

Encourage one another daily, as long as it is called To-day, so that none of you may be hardened by sin's deceitfulness *(Hebrews 3:13).*

Let us not give up meeting together, as some are in the habit of doing, but let us encourage one another—and all the more as you see the Day approaching *(Hebrews 10:25).*

But when used as a tactic, affirmation-on-demand becomes phony, and biblical affirmation has slipped over the line into manipulation. We must ask ourselves—What is the purpose of the tactic? Is the approval sincere? Is the motive pure? Is the end result to build up one another or to build a bigger power platform and gain a larger following? Any leader handing out biscuits to make a follower perform like a trained animal or to create unswerving loyalty to its master must introspectively search and repent of his or her self-serving intentions.

This textbook tactic is as old as the door-to-door vacuum cleaner salesman. People with any discernment at all immediately recognize a disingenuous spirit that is nothing more than flattery to achieve sought results. The real result is a loss of trust in the leader's personal integrity.

Authentic means "not false or imitation" according to *Merriam-Webster Online Dictionary.* The unquestionable evidence of our leadership authenticity will not be in our words. It will be in the integrity of our *being* and our *doing.* To use an old maxim, "The proof is in the pudding."

Holy leaders are authentic. Their character, ordained by God, is the same in the boardroom or the classroom, at home or in worship, behind closed doors or on the stage. Who they are at the core of their being is clear and constant, the same today as it was yesterday.

> We have renounced secret and shameful ways; we do not use deception, nor do we distort the word of God. On the contrary, by setting forth the truth plainly we commend ourselves to every man's conscience in the sight of God *(2 Corinthians 4:2)*.

Where actions and words are inauthentic, people are manipulated rather than encouraged. Steeped in an excess of secular leadership principles, some of us need to take a step back and ask ourselves a hard question: Where does my leadership stop looking like Jesus and start using people for self-seeking gain?

In every interaction with people, Jesus' goal was to bring heaven to earth through serving others. The driving force of His earthly ministry was to do the will of His Father. In each personal encounter, He sought only to give, never to receive. Even in the encounter with the Samaritan woman at the well, though He asked for a drink of water, His ultimate goal was to give.

> Jesus answered her, "If you knew the gift of God and who it is that asks you for a drink, you would have asked him and he would have given you living water" *(John 4:10)*.

Jesus built no platforms for an earthly kingdom. He offered no self-serving, hollow flattery. Rather, he was direct with people, asking them what they needed and seeking to meet their needs:

> Jesus stopped and called them. "What do you want me to do for you?" he asked. "Lord," they answered, "we want our sight." Jesus had compassion on them and touched their

eyes. Immediately they received their sight and followed him *(Matthew 20:32-34)*.

As He healed people, He sent them out with instructions to tell no one. He sought no glory for himself but only for His Father.

Then he touched their eyes and said, "According to your faith will it be done to you"; and their sight was restored. Jesus warned them sternly, "See that no one knows about this" *(Matthew 9:29-30)*.

For many, the line between manipulation and authenticity is so fine it becomes virtually invisible. But when we are sincerely seeking the guidance of the Holy Spirit, that fine line becomes a gaping chasm we cannot and will not breach. Holy leaders identify and articulate a Jesus-style motivation. In short, wherever we lead, we must "Remember Jesus."

Whatever you do, whether in word or deed, do it all in the name of the Lord Jesus, giving thanks to God the Father through him *(Colossians 3:17)*.

In this me-first motivated world of leadership off track, how can we emulate Jesus in a holy leadership style?

Start with God's Word. It seems obvious, but are we neglecting the obvious source in our leadership training?

When I was the director of our denomination's global missions support organization, we received word from Cuba, for which we had long prayed: the Communist government would allow us to bring Bibles to the people. Immediately I was contacted by our believers there: Could you help us get Bibles? Through a network, we worked quickly for several agencies to adopt this project. The Bibles were purchased and shipped to Cuba in time for the church's district assembly. The delivery time had arrived, and people respectfully lined up to receive this long-anticipated gift—their own personal copy of the Bible. Only a few of them had ever owned a Bible. One by one, as they received it, their joy was inexpressible. They embraced it. They kissed it. They ran their fingers over the pages while tears flowed down their cheeks. How thankful they were for their new most valued possession! How privileged we are to have His Word!

Most Americans own a Bible. The average number of Bibles per home is estimated at three. But how many of us are reading the world's quintessential leadership text?

In a competitive market, how can we distinguish ourselves from the get-ahead mentality of the crowd if we do not have the perspective of Jesus? How can we lead like Jesus if we are not thinking like Jesus? How can we have His mind-set if we are not wrapping ourselves in His Word?

> The word of God is living and active. Sharper than any double-edged sword, it penetrates even to dividing soul and spirit, joints and marrow; it judges the thoughts and attitudes of the heart *(Hebrews 4:12)*.

Martin Luther, the great Protestant reformer, said, "The Bible is alive. It speaks to me. It has feet. It runs after me. It has hands. It lays hold on me." The Word of God is not just another book. It is living and powerful. It is penetrating, cutting right to the heart of our motives and tactics. It exposes our self-seeking ways and reveals to us the honor of our leadership intentions and practices.

The Bible is inspired, the very literal breath of God. His Word is eternal, ageless, and unchanging. It corrects and convicts us. It points out our sins and will not let us hide our eyes from their revelation: "All Scripture is God-breathed and is useful for teaching, rebuking, correcting and training in righteousness" (2 Timothy 3:16).

Tangled in the challenges of daily living, the hectic leader is too busy handing down directives to receive divine direction, too busy evaluating and correcting others to be divinely rebuked, too caught up in training manuals to be divinely trained in righteousness. By contrast, the holy leader is *seeking* teaching, rebuking, correcting, and training by immersing himself or herself daily in God's Word.

J. I. Packer said, "The Bible is the rope God throws to us to ensure we stay connected while the rescue is in process." Even as His Word rebukes and convicts us, He is offering reconciliation and forgiveness.

Henry Blackaby, author of *Experiencing God*, said that 90 percent of the scripture on repentance is directed at the believer. Through the revelation of the Holy Spirit and God's Word, we will recognize when we do not have perfect communication or perfect performance. There is a place for repentance in the life of the Spirit-filled believer. There is a need for repentance in the lives of holy leaders.

If we are truly living in willing openness to God's inspection, we will find that we do more repenting after receiving Christ as Lord than before. Do we believe in a sinning religion? God forbid! But when our failures are revealed to us, when there is anything in our lives that needs the perfecting that only He can provide, we should not rest until we have confessed and sought forgiveness. As our leadership responsibilities increase, so should our sensitivity to the Holy Spirit's finger pointing out failings and faults. Blackaby said, "Confession is looking at God, then looking at ourselves, and talking out the difference." Prayer is praying out the difference so that we are inwardly transformed by God's grace and equipped for holy leadership service.

The Word of God guides us for every task in every leadership role: "All Scripture is God-breathed . . . so that the man of God may be thoroughly equipped for every good work" (2 Timothy 3:16-17).

Is there a place for leadership books and seminars for instructing the holy leader? Absolutely. But only in subordination to the divine Word of God. We need to grow in the knowledge of God's Word, using it to test every experience, lifestyle, doctrine, and teaching. Measure every leadership principle against the eternal standard of Scripture. Within leadership circles, there are many artificials, look-alikes, and wanna-bes in both the world and the Church. When we delve into God's Word, He will enlighten our minds and quicken our hearts. By the guidance of the Holy Spirit, we will recognize among popular leadership teaching what is scripturally authentic and what is artificial.

> If any of you lacks wisdom, he should ask God, who gives generously to all without finding fault, and it will be given to him *(James 1:5)*.

What this hectic world needs is holy leaders, steeped in the Scriptures and covered in prayer, armed with Spirit-fed wisdom to take the best from secular leadership principles and filter it through the Jesus-style.

The Bible speaks to every generation about every situation. John Wesley said, "If it's new, it isn't true. If it's true, it isn't new." The lifespan of the average book is about two years, but God's Word is eternal and will stand forever. The Jesus-style of leadership is as old as His Word. If you want to know more about God, look at His Son. Read His words. Model His character. Emulate His prayer life. Adopt His servanthood. In short, in all your leadership responsibilities, *remember Jesus.*

When we are faced with the family schism, the falling test scores, and the slumping sales figures, when we are tempted to resort to secular tactics to fix our world where in reality everything is spiritual, God will supply all our needs. We are invited to come boldly before the Lord, shoulders squared, head up. We are His children, given unlimited, 24/7 access to Him for help in every crisis.

Let us then approach the throne of grace with confidence, so that we may receive mercy and find grace to help us in our time of need *(Hebrews 4:16).*

When we have come to Him repeatedly with the same deficiencies and faults, when we begin to turn instead to other sources for help, instruction, or leadership, we must remember that He alone has all the grace and mercy we need. It is not what we can do or what we bring but rather who He is.

Not the labor of my hands
Can fulfill Thy law's demands;
Could my zeal no respite know,
Could my tears forever flow,
All for sin could not atone;
Thou must save, and Thou alone.

Nothing in my hand I bring,
Simply to the cross I cling;
Naked, come to Thee for dress;
Helpless look to Thee for grace;[3]

Before you try harder, work longer, or employ new strategies, before you degenerate into depending solely on your own wisdom, abilities, or efforts, remember: Jesus modeled for us all the answers. He is completely adequate for every situation in our lives.

My God will meet all your needs according to his glorious riches in Christ Jesus *(Philippians 4:19).*

There is nothing we can do to impress God, and there is nothing God cannot do to help us. His grace is best displayed in human weakness when we lead in the servant-model of His Son.

The Hebrews were tempted to trust in their Temple, their ceremonies, their priests, their sacrifices, their long flowing robes, and their eloquent prayers. We have a better way, a New Covenant, the Son of God as our High Priest. He is our Mediator, ever interceding for us.

He is our Emmanuel, God with us. Because He is God, He will be with us everywhere and never forsake us. Because He became man, He understands our infirmities. He saw people hungry and fed them. Awakened in the boat, he saw people afraid and calmed their storm. He saw people grieving, stopped their funeral procession, and raised the dead to life.

He understands what it means to lead people. He knows about half-hearted followers: "Another disciple said to him, 'Lord, first let me go and bury my father.' But Jesus told him, 'Follow me, and let the dead bury their own dead'" (Matthew 8:21-22).

He knows what it means to be unappreciated. "Jesus asked, 'Were not all ten cleansed? Where are the other nine? Was no one found to return and give praise to God except this foreigner?'" (Luke 17:17-18).

He knows what it means to work with uncooperative, difficult people. "'O Jerusalem, Jerusalem, you who kill the prophets and stone those sent to you, how often I have longed to gather your children together, as a hen gathers her chicks under her wings, but you were not willing'" (Matthew 23:37).

He knows what it means to be betrayed by your closest followers. "While they were reclining at the table eating, he said, 'I tell you the truth, one of you will betray me—one who is eating with me'" (Mark 14:18).

Yet He willingly sacrificed himself for all of them. This is the Jesus-style leadership.

Jesus experienced hunger, rejection, oppression, and loneliness. He knows what it means to be tempted, stressed out, tired, and grief-stricken. Jesus identifies with leaders of every century and every generation. He models for us the better way. He will never leave us, forsake us, mislead us, forget us, or overlook us. When we fall, He lifts us. When we fail, He forgives us. When we are lost, He is the Way. When we are afraid, He is our courage. When we stumble, He steadies us. When we are blind, He leads us. When we are hungry, He feeds us. When we face trials, He is our advocate. When we suffer loss, He comforts us.

What does it mean to lead in the Jesus-style? It means to lift, to forgive, to provide the way, to bolster courage, to steady, to feed, to advocate, to comfort. It means not to be served, but to serve (Matthew 20:28). It means to remember Jesus.

My life is too hectic, too hurried, too harried. It is under-budgeted, over-scheduled, and ultra-obligated.

I'm asked to do too much in too little time with inadequate resources, outdated equipment, and ill-prepared assistants.

My staff is over-rated, under-motivated, self-consumed, uninspired, uncaring, and unaware.

My team is off-balance, off-task, off-schedule, off-budget, and off-target.

My family is out of control, out of patience, directionless, loveless, and lawless.

I've read every leadership book, attended every parenting seminar, completed every personality profile, taken every self-improvement course, done the strengths-finder inventory, and persevered through every church growth conference I can find—yet I still feel inundated, inadequate, imperfect, unsuccessful, and unfollowed.

I desire to be child-molding, character-building, team-motivating, others-centered, Christ-lifting, and self-effaced—yet I find myself repeatedly demanding, berating, correcting, and criticizing.

So why does God continue to call me to be a leader?

The 1960 Olympics in Rome were a mere shadow of the media spectacle we have come to know with television covering multiple venues in real time around the world. In 1960, television played second to the print media. CBS sent only three on-site commentators to Rome. Tapes were flown daily from Rome to New York, where Jim McKay, a studio host, edited the tapes and wrote his own scripts for the broadcasts of events where winners had already collected their medals.

One of the most memorable events was the marathon, the quintessential Olympic event. As runners lined up for the race, one United States participant looked over at a "skinny little African guy in bare feet" and said, "There's one guy we don't have to worry about."

The race was grueling. Runners settled into their strategized packs. The first leg went along a stately Roman boulevard past grandiose state buildings and then out into the Italian countryside. A second shorter leg covered the outer beltway highway around Rome. As the race wore on, darkness fell, and unlike today's constant media-spectacle, there were no cameras, no spectators, not even any lights.

With fatigue setting in and darkness all around, many runners became disoriented. Separated from the pack, some wondered if they had missed a turn and were on the wrong path. Then one or two runners would pass them in the darkness, leaving them behind but providing some comfort that they were still on the right track.

The final leg turned off the highway and headed back north toward the city along the historic Appian Way, "queen of the Roman roads." The darkness gave way to semi-light up ahead as a thousand soldiers holding torches were stationed 10 meters apart like human streetlights, while a half-moon glowed over the uneven ancient cobblestones. The leading runners reached the row of cypress trees and ancient ruins off to the side when at last a golf cart, two motorcycles, and a station wagon carrying the film crew could be seen. Two runners approached them, and in the silence, the soundman in the back of the station wagon picked up the noise of footfalls along the centuries-old cobblestones. It was the bare feet of Abebe Bikila, a completely unknown Ethiopian athlete.

Despite the distance and the long hours, Bikila breathed lightly, exhibiting no signs of strain. The crowd pressed forward to see this unexpected participant cross the finish line, dancing in the shadow of the floodlit Arch of Constantine. This barefoot unknown had run the fastest marathon time in all of Olympic history.[4]

How had he done it? Running was a way of life to Abebe Bikila. He had run all his life in the mountains near Debre Berhan. W. H. Strang, a British national who had earlier worked in Ethiopia, wrote in a letter to the *Ethiopian Herald*,

> It is a common sight to see dozens of men running to market every day along the Jimma road, past the old airport buildings, carrying heavily loaded baskets above their heads. It is men such as these as well as those who run for miles behind their donkeys, who have demonstrated what reserves of power there must be in their bodies to enable them to run such long distances in such difficult circumstances. *There must be hundreds of Ethiopians with tremendous potentials of endurance.*[5]

Jesus called the most unlikely unknowns—the uneducated, the poor, those who had been passed over by other rabbis. He is calling you. "Remember Jesus." In the hectic conundrum of your daily life, you have the *tremendous potential of Spirit-led endurance*. Be a holy leader.

NOTES

Chapter 1

1. Wikipedia contributors, "Where's the beef?," *Wikipedia, The Free Encyclopedia*.

2. Mother Teresa to the Rev. Michael Van Der Peet, September 1979.

Chapter 2

1. J. I. Packer, *Christianity Today*, March 2008.

2. *Merriam-Webster Online Dictionary*, s.v. "call," <http://www.merriam-webster.com/dictionary/call>.

3. *Merriam-Webster Online Dictionary*, s.v. "predict," <http://www.merriam-webster.com/dictionary/predict>.

4. Andrew Young, Interview, April 4, 2008, NBC Today Show, <http://www.msnbc.msn.com/id/21134540/vp/23952104#23952104>.

5. Ibid.

Chapter 3

1. Thomas O. Chisholm, "O to Be Like Thee," in *Sing to the Lord* (Kansas City: Lillenas Publishing Co., 1993), 490.

Chapter 4

1. *Merriam-Webster Online Dictionary*, s.v. "corporate," <http://www.merriam-webster.com/dictionary/corporate>.

2. Ralph E. Hudson, "A Glorious Church," in *Sing to the Lord* (Kansas City: Lillenas Publishing Co., 1993), 672.

Chapter 5

1. http://www.divorcerate.org

Chapter 8

1. Dominic Rushe, "Black Narcissi," http://business.timesonline.co.uk, March 28, 2004

2. http://abcnews.go.com

3. Augustus M. Toplady, "Rock of Ages," in *Sing to the Lord* (Kansas City: Lillenas Publishing Co., 1993), 445.

4. David Maraniss, *Rome 1960: The Olympics That Changed the World*, (emphasis added by author)

5. Ibid.